Women Explorers

Sylvia Earle
Deep-Sea Explorer

Women Explorers

Women Explorers

Sylvia Earle
Deep-Sea Explorer

Susan Tyler Hitchcock

Introduction: Milbry Polk,
author of *Women of Discovery*

CHELSEA HOUSE
PUBLISHERS
A Haights Cross Communications Company

Philadelphia

CHELSEA HOUSE PUBLISHERS
VP, NEW PRODUCT DEVELOPMENT Sally Cheney
DIRECTOR OF PRODUCTION Kim Shinners
CREATIVE MANAGER Takeshi Takahashi
MANUFACTURING MANAGER Diann Grasse

Staff for SYLVIA EARLE
ASSOCIATE EDITOR Kate Sullivan
PHOTO EDITOR Sarah Bloom
PRODUCTION EDITOR Megan Emery
SERIES & COVER DESIGNER Terry Mallon
LAYOUT 21st Century Publishing and Communications, Inc.

A Haights Cross Communications ✈ Company

http://www.chelseahouse.com

First Printing

9 8 7 6 5 4 3 2 1

Library of Congress Cataloging-in-Publication Data

Hitchcock, Susan Tyler.
  Sylvia A. Earle : deep sea explorer / Susan Tyler Hitchcock.
    v. cm. -- (Women explorers)
  Includes bibliographical references (p.) and index.
  Contents: Taking a walk with Jim -- Pulled into the ocean, 1935-1952 -- Studying the underwater world, 1952-1963 -- Diving into marine biology, 1964-1969 -- The diver is a woman, 1970-1975 -- Diving adventures, human and otherwise, 1975-1980 -- The better to see the world underwater, 1980-1985 -- America's sturgeon general, 1985-1992 -- Hero of the planet, 1992-2003.
  ISBN 0-7910-7712-8
  1. Earle, Sylvia A., 1935---Juvenile literature. 2. Women explorers--United States--Biography--Juvenile literature. 3. Explorers--United States--Biography--Juvenile literature. 4. Underwater exploration--Juvenile literature. 5. Deep diving--Juvenile literature. 6. Women marine biologists--United States--Biography--Juvenile literature. 7. Marine biologists--United States--Biography--Juvenile literature. 8. Marine biology--Juvenile literature. [1. Earle, Sylvia A., 1935- 2. Marine biologists. 3. Scientists. 4. Underwater exploration. 5. Women--Biography.] I. Title. II. Series.
  GC65.H54 2004
  551.46'0092--dc22

                                              2003026137

Table of Contents

Introduction

By Milbry Polk

Curiosity is one of the most compelling forces of human life. Our desire to understand who and what and where we are drives us restlessly to explore and to comprehend what we see. Every historical era is known by the individuals who sought to expand our boundaries of time and space and knowledge. People such as Alexander the Great, Ibn Battuta, Marco Polo, Ferdinand Magellan, Hernando de Soto, Meriwether Lewis, William Clark, Charles Darwin, Sir Richard Burton, Roald Amundsen, Jacques Cousteau, Edmund Hillary, Tenzing Norgay, Thor Hyerdahl, and Neil Armstrong are men whose discoveries changed our worldview. They were explorers, leaders into the unknown. This series is about a handful of individuals who have been left out of the history books but whose feats loom large, whose discoveries changed the way we look at the world. They are women explorers.

WHAT MAKES SOMEONE AN EXPLORER?

The desire to know what lies beyond the next hill—the desire to explore—is one of the most powerful of human impulses. This drive makes us unique among the species with which we share our earth. Curiosity helped to impel our remote ancestors out of Africa. It is what spread them in waves throughout the world where they settled; curiosity helped them adapt to the many environments they encountered.

Myths of all cultures include the memories of early explorations. These myths were the means by which people explained to themselves and taught their children about life, about the world around them, and about death. Myths helped people make sense of the inexplicable forces of nature and the strangeness of new lands and peoples. The few myths and legends that have come down to us are the stories of early exploration.

What makes someone an explorer? The qualities required are not unique. We are born explorers. Every child, even in the crib, is reaching out, trying to understand, to take the measure of its own body, then its immediate surroundings, and we continue as we go through life to grasp ever-widening circles of experience and reality. As we grow up, we often lose the excitement of the child, the characteristic that supposedly gave Albert Einstein his ability to see the universe in a new way. What typifies the explorer is not losing this wonderful childlike curiosity. He or she still reaches out. Explorers are open minded—able to look at and accept what they see, rather than to fall back upon preconceived notions. Explorers are courageous, not just in facing physical danger, but also in having the courage to confront failure, ridicule, and laughter, and yet to keep on going. Above all, explorers have the ability to communicate. All insights, observations, and discoveries mean nothing to the wider community if they are not documented and shared. An explorer goes out into the world at some personal risk and discovers something of value and then shares that knowledge with his or her community. Explorers are leaders who look at the world in new ways and in doing so make breakthroughs that enrich all of our lives.

WOMEN EXPLORERS

Women, like men, have always been explorers. Typically in a "hunter-gatherer" society the men hunted animals while the women ventured far from the camps in search of other foods. Though their tasks were different, both were explorers. And, since such societies were almost constantly on the move, women were there for each voyage of discovery. But over time, as cultural groups became more settled, ideas began to change about the role of women in society. Women came to be restricted to the house, the shared courtyard, or the village and began to wear clothing that set them apart. By the time of the Middle Ages often the only way women in the Western world could travel was by going on pilgrimage. The trek to visit holy sites offered women one of the few opportunities to see new places, hear new languages, and meet different people. In fact, the first autobiography in the English language was written by a pilgrim, Margery Kempe (1373–1440), about her journeys throughout Europe and to the Holy Land.

Over time, women became formally excluded from exploration. Of course, some women did manage to find a way around the obstacles. Those who did venture forth went alone or in disguise and often needed men to help them. But their stories were not recorded in official histories; to find their stories one has to dig deep.

About three hundred years ago, the western worldview changed. Beginning in the 1700s, the scientific revolution began to change life for everyone in Europe. Men as well as women were swept up in the excitement to classify and understand every aspect of life on earth. Legions of people went to every corner of the world to see and record what was there. The spirit of adventure began to find new means of expression. New modes of transportation made movement around the world easier and new technologies made recording events and communication less expensive and more vivid.

The findings of these explorers were fascinating to the people back home. Wealthy individuals collected many of the strange insects, botanical specimens, native art, rocks, and other findings, brought back by the explorers into personal collections called Cabinets of Curiosities. These Cabinets of

Curiosities are the forerunners of our modern museums. The desire to collect the unusual financed expeditions, which in turn fostered public interest in exploration. The creation and spread of scientific and popular magazines with stories about expeditions and discoveries enabled the public to learn about the world. By the 1800s, explorers had the status of popular heroes in the public eye. The lure of the unknown gripped society.

Unlike men, women did not have support of institutions such as universities, museums, scientific societies, governments, and the military that sponsored and financed exploration. Until well into the twentieth century, many of these institutions barred women from participation, membership, and especially leadership. Women were thought capable of gathering things such as flowers or rocks for subjects to paint and draw, but men were the ones who studied them, named them, and published books about them. Most women, if they had any specialized education at all, gained it through private tutors. Men went to the university. Men formed and joined scientific societies and the exploring clubs. Men ran the governments, the military, and the press, and archived the collections. Universities and other cultural institutions were open only to the membership of men. Women were generally excluded from them. When these institutions sponsored exploration, they sponsored men. Women not only had to overcome mountains in the wild but also institutions at home.

In the 1800s women were not usually trained or taught academics. Instead, they learned sewing, music, and how to behave as a lady. A woman who managed to learn to write overcame great obstacles. Few managed to do it, but the same spirit that made women into explorers animated their minds in other ways. A few women learned to record what they were doing sufficiently well that at least some of their works have become classics of description and adventure.

Because of them, we know the little we do know about their lives and actions. As the nineteenth century progressed, more and more women were going out collecting, recording, and writing about faraway places. By the late 1800s more women were educated and those who traveled often wrote accounts of their journeys. So, now, in the twenty-first century, we are just beginning to learn about the unknown side of exploration—the women's story—from the accounts that lay buried in our archives.

And what a story it is. For example, one of the first modern women explorers was Maria Sybila Merian, who sailed to Surinam in 1699 at the age of 52. Not content to view the strange flora and fauna that were arriving back in Europe to fill the Cabinets of Curiosity, she wanted to collect and paint insects and animals in their native habitat.

Western women also faced societal obstacles; they generally could not go anywhere without a chaperon. So for a would-be woman explorer, a night in the wild spent in the company of a man who was not a close relative or her husband was unthinkable. And then there were the unsuitable clothes. In many parts of the early modern world it was punishable by death (as it was in Spain in the 1600s) or imprisonment (as it was in America well into the late 1800s) for women to appear in public wearing pants.

The heavy, layered dresses and tight corsets thought necessary for women made traveling very cumbersome. For example, when the Alps began to be climbed by explorers in the 1800s, a few women were caught up in the mania. The first two women to summit the Matterhorn climbed in skirts and corsets. The third woman, an American professor of Latin, Annie Smith Peck (1850–1935), realized the absurdity of leaping crevasses, climbing ice walls, and enduring the winds in a skirt. So, she wore pants. This created such a sensation in 1895 that the Singer Sewing

Machine Company photographed her and included a card with her in climbing gear with every machine it sold.

THE WOMEN EXPLORERS SERIES

When asked why he wanted to climb Mount Everest, George Mallory famously replied "Because it's there." Perhaps another explorer would answer the same question, "Because I don't know what is there and I want to find out."

Although we all have curiosity, what separates explorers is their willingness to take their curiosity further. Despite the odds, a lack of money, and every imaginable difficulty, they still find a way to go. They do so because they are passionate about life and their passion carries them over the barriers. As you will discover, the women profiled in this series shared that passion. Their passion gave them the strength to face what would seem to be insurmountable odds to most of us. To read their stories is more than learning about the adventure, it is a guide to discovering our own passions. The women in this series, Mary Kingsley, Gertrude Bell, Alexandra David-Néel, Annie Montague Alexander, Sue Hendrickson, and Sylvia Earle, all join the pantheon of explorers, the heroes of our age.

These six women have been chosen because their interests range from geographical to cultural exploration; from traversing the highest mountains to diving to the depths of the oceans; from learning about life far back in time to looking forward into the future. These women are extraordinary leaders and thinkers. They are all individuals who have braved the unknown and challenged the traditional women's roles. Their discoveries have had remarkable and profound effects on what we know about the world. To be an explorer one does not have to be wealthy or have multiple degrees. To be an explorer one must have the desire from within and focus on the destination: the unknown.

Mary Kingsley (1862–1900) was the daughter of an English Victorian gentleman-explorer who believed women did not need to be educated. Mary was kept at home and only tutored in German to translate articles her father wanted to read. But while he was away, she went into his library and educated herself by reading his books. She never married and followed the custom of her day for unmarried women by staying home with her parents. When her parents died she found herself alone—and suddenly free. She purchased a ticket to the Canary Islands with her inheritance. Once there, she learned about the Congo, then considered by the Europeans to be a terrifying place. When Kingsley decided to go to the Congo, she was warned that all she would find would be festering swamplands laced with deadly diseases and cannibals. Kingsley viewed that warning as a challenge. Having used up all her money on the ticket, she outfitted herself as a trader. She returned to the Congo, and in a wooden canoe she plied the tributaries of the Congo River, trading goods with the natives and collecting fish for the British Museum. She learned the languages of the interior and befriended the local tribes. She became an expert on their rich belief systems, which were completely unknown in Europe. Like many explorers, Mary Kingsley's knowledge bridged separate worlds, helping each understand and appreciate the other.

Gertrude Bell (1868–1926) was the daughter of a wealthy English industrialist. She had tremendous ambition, which she used to convince her parents to give her an education at a time when, for a woman, education was considered secondary to a good marriage. As a result of her intelligence and determination, she won one of the few coveted spots for women at Oxford University. After college, she did not know what to do. Girls of her class usually waited at home for a proposal of marriage. But after Bell returned home, she received an invitation from her uncle to visit Persia (modern-day Iran). Quickly, she set about learning Persian. Later she learned Arabic and begin her own archeological trips into the Syrian deserts.

When World War I broke out, Bell was in the Middle East. Her ability to speak the language, as well as her knowledge of the local tribes and the deserts from her archeological work, caused the British to appoint her to one of the most important jobs in the Desert War, that of Oriental Secretary. The Oriental Secretary was the officer of the embassy who was expected to know about and deal with local affairs, roughly what we call a political officer in an embassy. Bell played a major role in crafting the division of the Middle East into the countries we know today. She also founded the museum in Iraq.

Alexandra David-Néel (1868–1969) was performing in the Paris Opera when she married a banker. As she now had some financial freedom, she decided to act on her lifelong dream to travel to the East. Soon after she married, she sailed alone for India. She assured her husband she be gone only about 18 months; it would be 24 years before she would return home. Upon arriving in India she became intrigued with the Buddhist religion. She felt in order to understand Buddhism, she had first to master Tibetan, the language in which many of the texts were written. In the course of doing so, she plunged so deeply into the culture that she became a Buddhist nun. After several years of study, David-Néel became determined to visit the home of the spiritual leader of the Tibetan Buddhists, the Dalai Lama, who resided in the Holy City of Lhasa, in Tibet. This was quite a challenge because all foreigners were forbidden from entering Lhasa. At the age of 55, she began a long and arduous winter trek across the Himalayas toward Tibet. She succeeded in becoming the first Western woman to visit Lhasa. After returning to France, David-Néel dedicated the rest of her long life to helping Westerners understand the beauty and complexity of Buddhist religion and culture through her many writings.

A wealthy and restless young woman, Annie Montague Alexander (1867–1950) decided to pursue her interests in science and nature rather than live the life of a socialite in San Francisco. She organized numerous expeditions throughout the American West to collect flora, fauna, and fossils. Concerned by the rapid changes occurring due to the growing population, Alexander envisaged a time, all too soon, when much of the natural world of the West would be gone due to urbanization and agricultural development. As a tribute to the land she loved, she decided to create the best natural history museum of the American West. She actually created two museums at the University of California, Berkeley, in which to house the thousands of specimens she had assembled. In the course of her exploration, she discovered new species, seventeen of which are named for her. Though little known, Alexander contributed much to our knowledge of American zoology and paleontology.

Two women in this series are still actively exploring. Sue Hendrickson dropped out of high school and made a living by collecting fish off the Florida Keys to sell to aquariums. An invitation to go on an underwater dive trip changed her life. She became passionate about diving, and soon found herself working with archeologists on wrecks. Hendrickson was often the lead diver, diving first to find out what was there. She realized she had a knack for seeing things others missed. On land, she became an amber collector of pieces of fossilized resin that contained insects and later became a dinosaur hunter. While on a fossil expedition in the Badlands of the Dakotas, Hendrickson discovered the largest *Tyrannosaurus rex* ever found. It has been named Sue in her honor. Depending on the time of year, she can be found diving in the sunken ancient port of Alexandria, Egypt, mapping Spanish wrecks off Cuba's coastline, or in the high, dry lands of ancient forests hunting for dinosaur bones.

Sylvia Earle began her exploration of the sea in the early days of scuba. Smitten with the undersea world, she earned degrees in biology and oceanography. She wanted more than to just study the sea; she wanted to live in the sea. In the early 1970s, Earle was eager to take part in a project in which humans lived in a module underwater for extended periods of time for the U.S. Navy. Unfortunately, when the project was about to begin, she was informed that because she was a woman, she could not go. Undaunted, Earle designed the next phase of the project exclusively for women. This project had far-reaching results. It proved to the U.S. military that women could live well in a confined environment and opened the door for women's entry into the space program.

Earle, ever reaching for new challenges, began designing and testing submersibles, which would allow a human to experience the underwater world more intimately than anything created up to that time. Approaching age 70, her goal is to explore the deepest, darkest place on earth: the 35,800-foot-deep Marianas Trench south of Guam, in the Pacific Ocean.

The experiences of these six women illustrate different paths, different experiences, and different situations, but each led to a similar fulfillment in exploration. All are explorers; all have given us the gift of understanding some aspect of our world. All offer tremendous opportunities to us. Each of us can learn from them and follow in their paths. They are trailblazers; but many trails remain unexplored. There is so much unknown about the world, so much that needs to be understood. For example, less than 5 percent of the ocean has been explored. Thousands of species of plants and animals wait to be discovered. We have not reached every place on earth, and of what we have seen, we often understand very little. Today, we are embarked on the greatest age of exploration. And we go armed with more knowledge than any of the explorers who have gone before us.

What these women teach us is that we need explorers to help us understand what is miraculous in the world around us. The goal for each of us is to find his or her own path and begin the journey.

1

Taking a Walk with *Jim*

A VALUABLE PAYLOAD

You could feel the excitement and tension as crewmembers aboard the research vessel *Holokai* held their breath and watched a transport vehicle release *Star II,* a small submarine, into the blue water six miles off Makapuu Point on Oahu, Hawaii.

Star II was carrying a valuable payload. Strapped on its prow was a figure that looked vaguely human. White and bulbous and hard to the touch, the thing looked like a cross between a snowman and an insect. It stood more than six feet tall on clunky boot feet. Arms bulged out on each side. At their ends, instead of hands, two sets of shiny metal tools snapped and swiveled like Swiss Army knives. The thing had no neck or shoulders. Its body rose straight up into a broad dome. Four huge eyes gazed out: one forward, one up, one left, and one right. Strapped to its back was an instrument box, guaranteeing life support for the woman inside this deep-sea diving invention.

The diving suit was named *Jim,* and the woman inside was Sylvia Earle. It was October 19, 1979, and at age 44, Sylvia Earle had already spent more than 4,000 hours underwater, exploring the plants, animals, and habitats that abound in the sea. A marine biologist, she had taken more risks than most men or women would ever take, coming eye-to-eye with the environment she studied. Her passion for the underwater world drove her to try every way possible to become part of it. This historic Hawaiian dive would add one more item to her list of accomplishments: Sylvia Earle would become the first person to use the innovative one-person diving suit for the sake of science. By reaching a depth of 1,250 feet and walking alone, without any attachment to a ship that hovered above, she would accomplish the world's deepest untethered solo dive ever.

As she descended, Sylvia Earle gazed out the forward porthole and enjoyed the light show that nature provided. "Shafts of gold from the midday sun penetrated the upper few feet, but gradually the colors mellowed into blue infinity, deep indigo

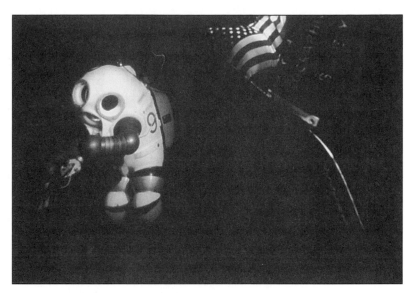

In 1979, after a weeklong process of learning to maneuver in the pressurized *Jim* suit, Earle spent two and a half historic hours exploring the ocean floor near the Hawaiian coast. She was walking 1,250 feet below the surface, untethered—a risk that no one had taken before—and only a thin communication line connected her to her colleagues on *Holokai* above. She planted an American flag on the sea floor to symbolize that exploring the oceans is just as important as exploring outer space.

shading to blue-black, the blue-edged darkness of deepest twilight or earliest dawn," Earle wrote in her book, *Sea Change.* "And there were stars, or so it seemed: small bioluminescent creatures sparkled with brilliant silver-blue flashes as they brushed against the pane through which I viewed Earth's 'inner' space."[1] Bioluminescence—the ability of plants and animals to glow from within, like fireflies—was one of the phenomena that most fascinated Sylvia Earle.

THE ADVANTAGES OF DIVING WITH *JIM*

Inside *Jim,* Earle could move around underwater for hours. It was a new and thrilling sensation. For most of her previous dives, she had used traditional scuba gear, wearing a skintight wetsuit and breathing compressed air through a regulator from tanks strapped to her back. With a scuba apparatus, she could stay underwater for about an hour and sometimes dive as deep as 150 feet from the surface. For long, deep dives, Earle had to allot time to allow her body to slowly return to surface pressure, a process known as decompression.

The gases that surround us on Earth exert one atmosphere of pressure (14.7 pounds per square inch) on our bodies at sea level. Water exerts more pressure, and the deeper a dive, the greater the pressure. For every 33 feet descended, the pressure increases by one atmosphere (see Appendix).[2] In other words, at 100 feet below the water's surface, the pressure on a diver's body is four times as forceful as that on land. That pressure influences not only flesh and muscle but also the gases in lungs, heart, and blood. For this reason, scuba divers have to pay meticulous attention to the mix of gases they breathe, to the time they spend underwater, and to the way they return to Earth's atmosphere. Coming up, they must allow time for their systems to readjust to surface pressure. Divers who resurface too quickly risk serious illness and even death, caused by the expansion of an excess of nitrogen gas bubbles in their bloodstreams.

A body-shaped submarine made of plastics and a magnesium alloy, *Jim* represented a way to bypass those restrictions. The suit was named for Jim Jarratt, a pioneering diver who wore a half-ton, armored "Iron Man" suit to dive 330 feet down off the coast of Ireland and discover the wreck of the *Lusitania* in 1935. The modern suit called *Jim* contained an atmosphere controlled to mimic that above the water's surface. *Jim*'s airflow system circulated a proper mix of air, chemically removing the carbon dioxide from exhaled breath. The suit's hard exoskeleton protected the person inside from the extremes of underwater pressure. All these features meant that a diver inside *Jim* could go deeper, stay longer, and return to the surface of the water more quickly and easily than those divers breathing compressed air.

For safety and mobility during her dive off Oahu, Sylvia Earle depended on others. Inside *Star II,* which delivered her to the ocean bottom, sat two key people. Bohdan Bartko piloted the craft, a classic little yellow submarine. Al Giddings, a photographer who had accompanied Earle on many dives, sat next to Bartko, filming the expedition through *Star II*'s portholes. For an extra measure of safety, Canadian engineer Phil Nuytten monitored the dive from the ship above. If necessary, he would dive down to rescue the mission, wearing another futuristic diving suit called *Wasp,* which used jet thrusters to fly through the water.

Jim was almost as experienced a diver as any of the humans accompanying him. The pressurized suit, originally developed in the late 1920s, had been modernized in the 1960s by a company called Oceaneering International. Used primarily by men working on oilrigs in the ocean, the suit had been lab tested and found to withstand pressures equal to those at 2,000 feet underwater. The deepest *Jim* had previously dived was 1,440 feet, when divers wore the suit to repair a broken cable off the coast of Spain. But in that case, as in all cases before Earle's dive in 1979, *Jim* always stayed attached to a mother ship by a tether. Sylvia Earle had no tether to the surface. Rather, she was linked to *Star II* by a light communication line, which would allow her to converse with Giddings and Bartko. It would also be the line by which *Star II* hauled *Jim* up to the water's surface at the end of the dive.

Earle had undergone a week of training to learn how to operate the diving apparatus. Because *Jim* was designed for men half a foot taller and nearly twice her weight, she had to compensate for her petite build. In just one week, as she described in her book *Exploring the Deep Frontier,* "I could walk, turn, lie down, get up, and even manage a modest, slow-motion cha-cha. I could manipulate Jim's two claws or leave my hands free for note taking. It was no more difficult, mechanically, than learning how to row a boat or ride a bicycle, and no more taxing physically."[3] If she wanted to look at something on the ocean bottom more closely, she had to use all the force of her body to throw *Jim* face down, landing horizontally. To get up again, she had to reverse the action. It helped that she had enough room inside the pressurized container to turn around and face backwards—something no husky man inside *Jim* could do.

AT HOME ON THE OCEAN FLOOR

That October morning in Hawaii, *Star II* and *Jim* slowly descended 1,250 feet and landed softly on the ocean bottom. Sylvia Earle looked out at the world that surrounded her. Its vast expanse overwhelmed her. "I abandoned for a moment all thoughts of the careful scientific evaluation I had planned," she wrote in *Sea Change*. "I simply enjoyed the sensation of being there, knowing that whatever might happen would be unlike anything I had ever experienced before—unlike anything *anyone* had ever experienced before."[4]

At 1,250 feet underwater, little sunlight penetrated, but spotlights loomed from *Star II*. In the glow of artificial light, Earle spotted a white sea sponge, soft and porous, attached to the ocean floor. Lacy coral stretched up into the deep blue water. A school of little red shrimp swam by, antennae taut and tails extended. Out of the corner of her eye, Earle glimpsed the snout of an eel. It poked into the light then retreated into the darkness.

Star II had landed at a relatively barren site. "I think it would be good to edge a little deeper and find more coral or a patch of rocks," Earle said to her chauffeurs.[5] She wanted to find a more interesting site before she committed herself to being unstrapped from her chariot. Once unstrapped, she could walk only a few yards from *Star II,* and she could not strap in again to try a different destination.

As Earle and *Jim* moved along the ocean bottom, an 18-inch shark loomed into view, staring at Earle with eerie green eyes. Soon they found a spot populated with slender spirals of bamboo coral, clumps of sponges, and fields of fan-like corals, all bending slightly in response to a swift current that flowed along the ocean floor. Intricate bouquets of gorgonian sea coral moved ever so slightly in the ripples caused by the submersible as it moved toward them. _Star II_'s light attracted a clutch of rays, which glided up toward it and then just as peacefully glided away. These creatures had no reason to fear the presence of humans.

At a signal from Earle, Giddings released the strap holding _Jim_ to _Star II_. With eager anticipation, Earle stepped out into this unknown world. She almost fell head over heels. One toe would not come loose from the submersible. In an anxious moment, she saw herself, toe stuck, being dragged up to the surface, her mission unfulfilled. Luckily, Bohdan Bartko had had thousands of hours of underwater piloting experience, and a quick jerk backward loosened _Jim_. With slow, deliberate steps, Sylvia Earle began her underwater exploration.

SYLVIA EARLE'S DISCOVERIES

All that Sylvia Earle saw that day was brilliant, beautiful, and awe-inspiring. For the first span of her two and a half hours in the Hawaiian depths, Earle made detailed observations, probed polyps, counted crabs, tracked shrimp, and followed jellyfish, keeping notes in her logbook and talking all the while to Al Giddings, who was filming her explorations for a planned television special.

A garden of tall, spiraling bamboo coral caught her eye. Earle reached out with her right-hand claw, the closest _Jim_ had to fingers, and grasped one small piece of coral to inspect later when she had returned to the surface.

Frustrated with her own claws, Earle felt a pang of envy when she saw a pale crab not too far away. She admired it, "gracefully tiptoeing along the sea floor while holding high a

The *Jim* suit enabled Earle to dive ten times as deep as was possible with ordinary scuba equipment, and her explorations in the suit revealed a world that no human had seen before. When she asked that her submersible's lights be turned off, she saw a world beyond that—one that glowed with eerie bioluminescence. Among her more unusual discoveries were the "fiery blue doughnuts" that moved serenely along the tall strands of bamboo coral. The coral (shown here) is named for its black-and-white segmentation, which resembles the structure of bamboo.

bouquet of gorgonian coral in each of its two small, hindmost pincers." Then she mused:

> Several kinds of deep-sea crabs have this habit, and while the reasons for such behavior are completely mysterious, I thought with a wry smile that a perceptive crab might be equally puzzled about the interest the strange upright creature awkwardly roaming in its territory might have in the wisp of coral _it_ held.[6]

Never one to call any underwater inhabitants strange, Sylvia Earle instead had developed a refreshing capacity to look at herself and the human world through sea creatures' eyes.

A four-inch, silvery lanternfish entered the sphere of light, its large, round, black eyes unaccustomed to such brilliance. Earle could see the photophores, or light-producing organs, lined up along the fish's body, but the sub's lights spoiled any chance to see the lanternfish's luminesce, and Earle asked her dive mates to turn them off so that she could experience the natural darkness of the sea 1,250 feet under the surface. She wrote of the experience:

> I waited for my eyes to adjust to what I expected to be total, absolute darkness. But no! Looking upward through _Jim_'s topmost port, I could see an immense amphitheater of blue-blackness arching over deep gray-blackness. Midday sunlight was apparent even to my eyes and would be magnified many times over for creatures whose senses are tuned for living at the edge of light. I could make out irregular shapes—sponges and clumps of low, branching coral, and the rounded hulk of the sub, 20 feet away. I was at the edge of darkness, that elusive, almost-dark-almost-light realm, the twilight zone.[7]

Once her eyes adjusted to the darkness, Earle found herself

in the habitat she wanted to witness: the underwater world of bioluminescence. Now the lanternfish glowed, its photophores emitting a bluish light. Now she could see the tiny hatchetfish, mostly head and with little body, barely an inch long. While their eyes seemed to point upward, their photophores cast blue light downward in a tactic presumed by marine biologists to disguise them from predators. Earle kept an eye out for other bioluminescent creatures she had studied but never seen, such as the deep-sea squid that defends itself by squirting out ink that glows.

With her eyes peeled for swimming creatures, Earle had not even looked closely at the bed of bamboo coral next to her. Brushing by these spiral strands, many taller than she was, she now noticed that the slightest touch sent rings of blue light pulsing down each stalk. When she touched the base, rings pulsed upward. "Would they cancel each other out?" she asked herself. She recorded her findings in *Sea Change*: "Serenely, the miniature fiery blue doughnuts merged, then each passed through the other and continued onward, apparently unperturbed by what appeared to me to be a setup for a truly scintillating encounter."[8]

BACK UP FOR AIR

Questions tumbled through Sylvia Earle's mind as she observed the coral's responses to her touch. What is the evolutionary advantage of luminescence to coral? Does the blue light fend off fish about to eat the coral like a "deep-sea burglar alarm"?[9] A bed of coral is made of many individual polyps, so does the entire colony ever participate in this colorful tactic? What bioluminescent light shows might take place when no human being is watching?

Throughout Earle's dive to the Hawaiian seafloor, every creature that presented itself, whether anchored to the bottom, drifting by, or whizzing out of view, raised an equally lengthy set of questions. Earle had only two and a half hours underwater. She understood that the purpose of this research dive was not to find answers but to bring back samples, observations, notes, and pictures—in other words, to raise new questions.

Back among her scientific colleagues, Earle found a curiosity that matched her own. She had done what no scientist had done before. To learn more about the deep ocean bottom, she had actually walked there and observed it, and everyone aboard *Star II* wanted to know what she had found there. "What did you see?" "Were you afraid?" "What's it like down there?" they asked. She did her best to answer but knew that no words, or even pictures, could convey the experience she had just had.

The excitement over, Earle returned home, eager to reunite with her three children, Elizabeth, 13; Richie, 11; and Gale, 5. She walked into the kitchen amid cheers and hugs and kisses. She was thankful that she had a family that trusted and respected her enough to let her go so far and so deep on her own.

When the hugging slowed down, she took a deep breath and looked around. She was glad to be home. Then she noticed, magneted to the refrigerator, the centerfold from *The Star,* a supermarket tabloid. There was a picture of her in a dive mask. Above the picture ran a bold headline in inch-high lettering—"Brave Mom's History Dive to the Bottom of the World."

Earle flinched. To think that she, a marine biologist and mother of three children, would appear in such a paper, alongside sex scandals, UFOs, and Hollywood divorces! Soon, however, she was laughing along with her children. The whole world was cheering her on. Although Earle understood that her Hawaiian dive had made history, she also knew it was just one small step toward the day when human beings would come to know and respect the vast world of life underwater.

2

Pulled into the Ocean
1935–1952

The best way to observe fish is to become a fish.
—Jacques-Yves Cousteau

GROWING UP NATURALLY

Sylvia Earle was always a child of the natural world. Her parents both grew up on farms, and although her father worked as an engineer for the DuPont Corporation, he and his wife raised their children with the farmer's sense of the value of the land, its plants, and its animals. Sylvia grew up with two brothers, one two years older and the other four years younger. Four older brothers had died before she could remember, one by accident and three from illness. Their deaths did not diminish the love that permeated the Earle household. "My parents really made me feel special, made me feel loved," Earle recalled. "I always felt, even as a small child, that I couldn't do anything so bad that I couldn't come home. . . . Somebody would take me in their arms and I would be reassured that it would be okay."[10] The Earle home was also filled with activity and passionate curiosity about the world.

When Sylvia was three years old, her family moved into an old brick farmhouse in the countryside south of Camden, New Jersey. Built at the time of the American Revolution, the house was nearly 200 years old, and it felt like part of the landscape. "We had squirrels and raccoons, and so many birds—the sky filled with birds, as I haven't seen them since," Earle told a writer from the *New Yorker* magazine in 1989.[11] She and her brothers considered the nearby woods their playground.

Once, her mother captured a shiny gold frog and clasped it gently in her hands. All three children clustered around and touched its soft belly. Sylvia especially wanted to hold it. After a few minutes, her mother said it was time to take it back to the pond where it lived. Sylvia carried it ceremoniously and placed it with great care at the edge of the pond, watching with delight as it leaped gracefully back into its own element.

Sometimes she and her brothers would go out in the

evening and catch fireflies. It was easy to catch the little beetles as they hovered eye-level in the midsummer twilight. Sylvia liked to cup them in her hand and peek inside to see how each insect's abdomen changed from dull gray to phosphorescent yellow.

Sometimes her mother would find a fuzzy caterpillar crawling on the ground near the garden. She would coax it onto her hand then let it crawl daintily across to Sylvia's. She taught Sylvia to hold still and respect the little living creature, not to poke it or prod it but to let it feel safe. Sylvia felt the tickle of its bristles as it crept across the back of her hand. "I learned very early on that if you show respect for other creatures, they won't go out of their way to harm you," Earle said, recalling the important lessons of her childhood.[12]

Thinking back on those early days, Sylvia Earle was especially thankful that her mother had taught her to approach nature with fascination, care, and concern:

> I really owe a lot of my interest in wild things to my mother. She just had a natural rapport with the world around her. Unlike a lot of parents, she would never say, "Yuk! Don't touch that slimy thing!" Instead, she'd bring a snake into the house and say, "Isn't this an elegant creature? Touch it gently, because it's very sensitive." And it wasn't zoology, at least not in any formal way. It was just an empathy for life.[13]

As an adult, Sylvia came to understand that the fear between human beings and the creatures of the natural world was a learned response—whether it meant humans recoiling at the sight of a snake or a spider or, conversely, the instinct of a bird or a deer to flee at the sight of a human. Whenever she dived in waters where no human being had ever been before, the creatures were naturally curious. They swam up to her and around her without any

Even in her childhood, Earle was an eager explorer of nature—first in the woods near the New Jersey farm on which she was raised, occasionally on the New Jersey coast, and then on the beaches of Florida. It was on the beach that she discovered the fascination with marine life that would fuel her later career. She earned a scholarship to Florida State University and worked in laboratories throughout her college years. This photograph was taken when Earle was about five years old.

sign of fear. They confirmed her belief that "the natural thing is to express the curiosity that is inherent in most young things." [14]

TAKING PLEASURE IN STUDY

Sylvia Earle was a naturally studious young person. She sat for hours in a willow tree at the edge of the pond, observing all that went on around her. She avidly watched thunderstorms as they formed and grew in the distance. On stormy afternoons, her mother insisted that she stay inside, but Sylvia pressed her nose against the window, getting as close as she could to the trees around her house. She loved the way they stirred and swayed in the winds at the leading edge of the storm. On sunny days, Sylvia would patiently sit at the pond's edge and catch fish, tadpoles, and frogs. She brought them home for observation and then carefully returned them to the places where they belonged. She wrote down her observations, made sketches, and kept notebooks of all she was finding. "Nobody had to *tell* me to do those things," she recalled. "I just did them. And I always *knew,* somehow, that I was going to be a biologist or a botanist or something, even before I knew what those things were called." [15]

With such a natural inclination to study, Sylvia went to school early, starting first grade at the age of five. At every stage of her education, she was younger than her classmates, and she graduated from high school at the age of 16. "I was like a big sponge, absorbing as much as I could," she once said. She even read the encyclopedia for enjoyment. She was also pleased that she was able to learn the intricacies of mathematics:

> I liked it when I could get my mind around the math problems. It was a sense of accomplishment that I could figure things out. It was the joy of success. Like a flash of light in your brain, an insight that you have derived from getting this piece of information and that piece of information,

and put them together, and independently come up with something else. I never tire of that kind of joy.[16]

Books fascinated Sylvia almost as much as did the phenomena of nature. She enjoyed science fiction and remembers the flights of fancy that she took after reading H. G. Wells's famous novel *The Time Machine*. "It was exhilarating to imagine traveling into the past or future as easily as taking a trip to the beach," Earle wrote in *Sea Change*. She tried to imagine the familiar places of her landscape as they might have looked 100 or 1,000 years before. What did her pond look like a century ago? What did the woods look like an eon ago? Even a generation ago things were different:

> My father described the Delaware River as a magical place ringing with the laughter of summer swimmers, a place filled with clear water and large fish that watched small boys with apparent curiosity. It did not sound at all like the Delaware River I knew as a child, a place already reeling from upstream pressures that forever changed the nature of that once immensely productive waterway.

Sylvia became vividly aware, early on in her lifetime, of the speed of the changes happening in the world. She was not always comfortable with the way things changed and was sometimes nostalgic about how things had been in the past:

> My parents, born in 1900 and 1902, grew up on small farms still surrounded by woodland, where flocks of birds darkened the skies, spring and fall. They had twenty kinds of apples, Seckel pears, garden corn, beans, and tomatoes every summer; fresh bread baked at home every day, hand-pumped well water, milk from their own cows, chestnut trees, and snow and rain that fell wondrously pure, without a deadly cargo of exotic hitchhiking chemicals.

The changes that occurred during the twentieth century were what most people termed "progress"—household electricity, indoor plumbing, cars and highways, airplanes and jets, radio and television, antibiotics, nuclear power, satellites, electronics, and computers. As Earle put it, progress also included "thousands of elements of everyday life that my children simply take for granted as a natural part of being a human being." [17] Molded by her outdoor upbringing and her reading, Sylvia viewed things differently.

THE LURE OF THE OCEAN

For vacations, the Earle family went to the New Jersey shore. It was close enough to their home that the trip was not a huge endeavor, but it was far enough that the journey was special every time. They would pack up the family car and drive through the New Jersey Pine Barrens to the sand dunes on the coast. "Before we could see or hear the ocean, we could smell it," Sylvia Earle remembers. "And then hear it. And then finally, there it was, this great incredible expanse. . . . I can still feel that leap of enthusiasm, and real joy, at the prospect of finally getting out to the beach, and running around." [18]

The freedom of running along the beach, the taste and feel of the salt in the air, the power of the crashing waves topped with frothy green were wonderful; everything about the ocean pulled Sylvia in and called to her. Other children might be frightened by the force of a wave that knocked them down and drew them under, but Sylvia laughed. She loved the power of the ocean. She was a natural swimmer, and adults, watching the way she held her hands against her sides and glided through the water, likened her to a tadpole.

Ocean creatures fascinated her. Crabs scuttled across the sand. Starfish lay revealed at the water's edge. Jellyfish gleamed, tossed on the sand by a wave. Intertwined strands of red and brown seaweed, strewn along the beach at the high tide line, suggested the shapes and colors of an under-water jungle.

Occasionally Sylvia was at the New Jersey shoreline when a fleet of horseshoe crabs scrambled ashore to reproduce. Horseshoe crabs are one of the four species in the class Merostomata.[19] With their flat, dome-shaped, hard shells, they resemble giant brown ladybugs. Long, barbed protuberances stick out behind, and young Sylvia Earle considered these "a convenient handle with which to pick them up for a closer look." Adults would worry that she was going to hurt herself, but Sylvia was more concerned about the horseshoe crabs. She considered it her duty—as with the fish and frogs from her backyard pond—to return them to the water:

> I gathered as many members of the gleaming brown armada as I could and turned them back into the sea—not aware that I was intruding on a vital ritual of mating: the release of eggs and sperm in the wave-washed inter-tidal area. It did not occur to me then that these enchanting creatures would one day bring into sharp focus the devastating impact one species—mine—is having on the future of life in the sea, and on the planet as a whole.[20]

As her career as a marine biologist evolved, Earle saw fewer and fewer of these creatures. She thought back fondly to the days when hundreds of horseshoe crabs would climb out of the ocean in her presence; the contrast became a symbol of the devastation of the ocean life she was so passionately determined to protect.

JOINING THE TRADITION OF OCEAN LOVERS

To learn more about ocean life, young Sylvia Earle began reading the true-life adventures of naturalist and explorer William Beebe. Beebe was a pioneering ecologist who helped establish the New York Zoological Society. He traveled all over the world, studying animals and bringing live specimens back to the zoo in New York. In 1928, he and inventor Otis Barton made a record underwater descent enclosed in Barton's new *Bathysphere,* a spherical metal diving vessel. During a highly publicized dive in the ocean near Bermuda, they went half a mile, or 3,028 feet, underwater.

In *Beneath Tropic Seas: A Record of Diving Among the Coral Reefs of Haiti,* William Beebe described an expedition to Haiti, sponsored by the New York Zoological Society in the 1920s. From the very first page, his feelings and views engaged Sylvia's imagination. "You are standing on a metal ladder in water up to your neck," Beebe's book began. "Something round and heavy is slipped gently over your head, and a metal helmet rests upon your shoulders." In Beebe's day, an underwater diver wore a hard helmet attached to a waterproof suit. On board a ship above, a fellow explorer pumped air through a hose and into the helmet, allowing the diver to breathe. Beebe's description of the diving experience fascinated Sylvia:

> As you descend, your diving globe now in place, you see emerald waves breaking upon the distant beach of ivory, backed by feathery palms waving in the sunlight against a sky of pure azure.
>
> You wave good-by to your grinning friend at the pump, and slowly descend, climbing down step by step. For a brief space of time the palms and the beach show intermittently through waves which are now breaking over your very face. Then the world changes. There is no more harsh sunlight, but delicate blue-greens with a fluttering of shadows everywhere. Huge pink and orange growths rise on all sides—you know they are living corals. . . . The first little people of this strange realm greet you—a quartet of swimming rainbows—four, gorgeously tinted fish who rush up and peer in at you.[21]

Thanks to Beebe's science adventure stories, Sylvia's worldview expanded. The natural world did not just consist of fields and forests, ponds, and the seashore. An entire underwater world lay waiting for her to explore it, full of color and shapes, plants and animals.

With her growing enthusiasm for underwater life, twelve-year-old Sylvia Earle must have felt excited when she learned that her family was moving from New Jersey to the west coast of Florida near Tampa Bay. Now the Gulf of Mexico would be her backyard. In 1948, the family moved to Dunedin, a small town outside Clearwater, Florida, where Lewis Earle, Sylvia's father, established his own electrical business. Sylvia attended high school and spent her free time reading and exploring. She traded hills and forests for salt marshes and sea grass beds, frogs and squirrels for sea horses and sea urchins.

Her concern over the changing environment of the ocean deepened when she read the book *The Sea Around Us.* Written by Rachel Carson, a protégée of William Beebe's, and published in 1951, the book stayed on America's bestseller lists for more than a year. It was simultaneously a natural history of the ocean, an appreciation of those people who had dedicated their lives to exploring it, and a plea for greater respect and care for the world's waters. A decade later, Rachel Carson would once again fascinate and unsettle the consciences of American readers with her book *Silent Spring,* which many consider the first trumpet call for environmentalists of the twentieth century.

At about the same time that she was reading Carson's book, an article in *National Geographic* magazine captured Sylvia Earle's imagination. It was written by Jacques-Yves Cousteau, who had much in common with her hero, William Beebe. Little known in those days, Cousteau had just renovated a retired World War II minesweeper named *Calypso,* transforming it into a floating research laboratory. During the war, he had used an Aqualung, a device that regulated airflow to

Earle has never stopped chasing the creatures that fascinated her on the beaches of her youth—like this jellyfish in the Florida Keys. "If you want to observe a fish," Earle once wrote, quoting the legendary Jacques-Yves Cousteau, "you must become a fish." She has spent four decades doing just that—meeting sea life below the surface, on its own terms, and designing vehicles to explore ever greater depths of the world's oceans.

individuals underwater, the first modern scuba diving gear. In the article, Cousteau was promoting the Aqualung for use in exploration.

"A Man-made Lung Gives This Diver an Hour's Permit to Explore the Twilight Sea," read one photo caption in his October 1952 article. Cousteau began his article by writing, "The best way to observe fish is to become a fish. And the best way to become a fish—or a reasonable facsimile thereof—is to don an underwater breathing device called the Aqualung. The Aqualung frees a man to glide, unhurried and unharmed, fathoms deep beneath the sea."[22] The description must have seemed irresistible to Sylvia. More than likely, she imagined how delightfully the Aqualung could free a woman, too.

THE PHYSICS OF DIVING

One of the most important lessons a scuba diver learns is to come back up to the water's surface slowly. It can be a matter of life and death.

Human bodies are accustomed to the pressure exerted by gases in the open atmosphere. Average air pressure at sea level is 14.7 pounds per square inch (see Appendix), also referred to as "one atmosphere" of pressure. As human beings ascend into space—whether climbing mountains or riding in space vehicles—the air pressure lessens. As human beings dive underwater, the air pressure increases. Sylvia Earle likes to demonstrate this principle by holding up a tiny Styrofoam cup on the end of her index finger—a piece of trash she brought up from a 1,000-foot-deep dive. Once a standard-sized cup, it was compacted by underwater pressure.

Human bodies experience that same force underwater. Of greatest concern is the effect of underwater pressure on the gases inside the human respiratory and circulatory systems. On land, humans breathe a combination of gases, oxygen and nitrogen chief among them. When the body undergoes increased pressure, its tissues absorb more than the ordinary amount of gases, especially nitrogen. At 50 feet underwater, for example, even when a diver breathes air from scuba tanks normally, nitrogen in the organs and blood stream builds to levels higher than normal.

As the diver ascends, the nitrogen level in the bloodstream naturally decreases, but very slowly. Divers must pace them-selves as they swim back up, so that the rate of ascent matches the rate of nitrogen level reduction. Otherwise, the excess nitrogen bubbles up, just like soda in a shaken bottle. Bubbles clog blood vessels, joints, and organs, causing a painful and life-threatening condition called decompression sickness or "the bends," a nickname that describes how a diver's limbs collapse when suffering from the condition.

THE FIRST DIVE

With all these exciting ideas filling her imagination, Sylvia's life took a sudden turn "downward," as she wrote in *Sea Change*. A next-door neighbor, Earle wrote, "borrowed his father's copper diving helmet, compressor, and pump, and introduced several of his pals, including Skip [her brother] and me, to the fine art of breathing underwater."[23] She put on the helmet, which linked her by tube to compressed air tanks on land, and lowered herself into the Weekiwatchee River. She felt the pain of increased pressure in her ears and swallowed a few times to equalize the pressure. When she felt the river bottom with her feet, she knew she was 30 feet underwater.

The first creature she saw was an alligator gar—a long, bony, flat-snouted river fish that can grow longer than a human being can grow tall. Sylvia watched with wonder—not fear—as the gar exercised its jaws, showing its four rows of teeth. Then the fish slowly turned and swam away, as unperturbed as the teenaged girl watching it. Despite the ungainly equipment she was wearing, Sylvia had a knack for joining the underwater world without disturbing it:

> From the fishes' standpoint, I was a noisy apparition of rushing bubbles, hose, and huge helmet with legs, but I willed myself to be inconspicuous and, as stealthily as I could, made my way toward them. Then, something totally unexpected happened. First one, then several, and finally all of the small fish I had been stalking turned and swam in my direction. I was supposed to be the watcher, but found myself the *watchee*, the center of attention for a bunch of curious fish, apparently mesmerized by the strange bubbling being that had just fallen through their watery roof. For twenty blissful minutes, I became one with the river and its residents . . .[24]

When Sylvia surfaced from this first diving experience, her whole sense of her future had shifted. She had found a fascinating, challenging, and inviting world. It was a world in which she felt at home. She had one burning question on her mind: How could she work it so that she could go underwater all the time?

3

Studying the
Underwater World
1952–1963

UNIVERSITY-BOUND

When Sylvia Earle graduated from high school in 1952, she was sure of two things: She wanted to continue her education, and she wanted to keep diving. In fact, she wanted to find a way to do both at the same time. Her parents could not afford to completely pay her way through college, so Earle helped support herself. She spent a year taking classes at St. Petersburg Junior College, near home, and received an associate of arts degree. Then she was admitted, with working scholarships, to Florida State University in Tallahassee, more than 200 miles from home.

It was a large university that offered many courses, but Earle had a good idea of what she wanted to study. She just had to find the right people to teach her. The professor who made all the difference was a man named Harold Humm. In 1949, Humm had established a research program in oceanography at Florida State. He recognized that understanding the world of the ocean well meant bringing together many different scientific viewpoints, and his students learned biology, chemistry, geology, meteorology, and physics. For someone like Sylvia Earle, whose enthusiasm for learning went in many directions, it was a good fit.

She embarked on projects based at one of the three Florida State oceanography field stations, spending as much time at the Alligator Harbor Marine Laboratory on the Gulf of Mexico near Appalachicola Bay as she did in any classroom. "My professor, Dr. Harold J. Humm, made it clear that he thought the best way to study fishes was to go where the fishes were, to meet them on their own terms," Earle wrote.[25] For her, that was simply an invitation to do just what she wanted to do. In those days, few scientists had used underwater diving equipment to study the ocean environment. College student Sylvia Earle was one of the first to do so.

DEEP IN HER STUDIES

"In the early days of scuba diving, as in the early days of aviation, no one had a license," recalled Sylvia Earle in her book *Sea Change.*

> Those who were so inclined figured out the dos and don'ts for themselves or learned by watching someone else who had done so. Nowadays, a person who wants to try scuba can readily find places to take a course and compress the years of trial and error by the pioneers into a week or so of training. No such courses existed in 1953, however, when I was first given a chance to realize my dream of diving with an Aqualung while taking a class in marine biology— My professor, Harold Humm—provided us with several ways to view the action: glass-bottomed buckets, face masks and flippers, a Desco mask—a full-face system with about 100 feet of air hose connected to a surface air compressor—and, best of all, two gleaming new air tanks equipped with double-hose regulators.[26]

Of course, Earle tried them all, but with scuba, she could go the deepest with the most independence. From a boat five miles from shore, Earle descended for her first scuba dive. She had read and listened. She knew the dangers and she anticipated the thrills, but nothing was like really doing it. The procedures involved in the descent and the steady breathing came naturally. "With a gentle kick I glided to a small clump of sponges and found a feisty three-inch-long damselfish who was not pleased by my intrusion into its territory," she wrote later. She had seen fish like these before—wearing a mask and holding her breath underwater—but what a difference the breathing apparatus made for the sake of observation. "Now I could stay, waiting and watching, until the fish became relaxed and went about its business."[27]

She experimented with the feeling of being underwater,

The many happy days she'd spent on the beaches of New Jersey and Florida helped Earle to choose her path in college. Once she'd discovered the freedom of diving—moving like a dolphin, but without having to return frequently to the surface for air—her desire to explore became a passion. She studied every diving method she could and became one of the first women to use scuba gear. Later in her career, she began to create vehicles to increase human dexterity in the ocean.

discovering how to use weights to counteract her body's buoyancy and to enjoy the freedom of diving without any attachments tethering her to the surface. She could tip upside down and stand on one finger and, from this vantage point, peer into the chinks in the coral where fishes hid. She could roll backwards in a midwater flip, as fluid as a jellyfish. She could swim upside down, then U-turn to the bottom, 20 feet below the water's surface. "The fish were almost certainly perplexed by the large mass thrashing about in their midst," wrote Earle, "but in my mind I was dolphinlike—but with an edge on the dolphins. They have to surface to breathe every few minutes, but with the air tank I could stay submerged for an hour." [28] Sylvia Earle had found her element.

TO STUDY PLANTS IS TO STUDY LIFE

The obvious thing for someone interested in marine biology to

EARLY DIVING INVENTIONS

Staying underwater is a quest that has challenged humans for thousands of years. Early diving efforts depended on the same physical laws that can be demonstrated by turning a glass upside down and pressing it straight down into a bucket of water. Tilt it and a bubble rises, proving that air has been trapped inside. Ancient Greek divers dropped kettles upside down in the water with them, providing a little more air to extend their time underwater.

In the late 1600s, Edmond Halley—the same man of comet fame—designed a wooden diving chamber sealed with lead and big enough for a man to sit inside. It sank to the sea bottom, tethered to a boat above and held down by weights on the ocean floor. Barrels, pumped full of air on board the ship, were weighted and sent underwater to replenish the air in the chamber. A pilot remained inside the chamber and divers walked the ocean floor nearby. They wore hemispherical helmets. Air was piped into the helmets from the wooden chamber, providing a small breathing reservoir. One diving venture using Halley's method 50 feet below water surface lasted nearly two hours.

In 1715, John Lethbridge, an English inventor, climbed into a body-length oak barrel, an early full-body diving suit. He stuck his arms into leather sleeves fastened to the barrel and gazed out a glass window sealed at one end. Just over 100 years later, in 1819, Augustus Siebe perfected a diving suit tight enough that air could be pumped down through tubes into the helmet for breathing.

As primitive as all these efforts seem to twenty-first-century readers, who are accustomed to a world of scuba and submarines, they were brave and necessary steps in the evolution of the equipment that has allowed human beings to spend time in the underwater world.

study is fish—or maybe marine mammals, such as dolphins or whales. Sylvia Earle took a different route. She saw the passion with which Professor Humm approached algae, and she decided to concentrate on ocean plants as well.

Most people consider algae just green scum. Earle came to look on algae as one of the world's most complicated, fascinating, beautiful, and important forms of life—from single-celled forms with a structure visible only under the microscope to massive seaweeds that stretch their fronds 100 feet or more up from the ocean bottom and sometimes grow a foot a day. Life on Earth depends on algae, voluminous masses of plant material that photosynthesize and create food at the bottom of the food chain. Without algae, the world of plants, animals, and human civilization would not be what it is today.

In Earle's educated view, algae symbolized the role that all plants play on Earth. "If you study plants you look at everything—geology, chemistry of the environment," she once told a reporter from the *New York Times Magazine*. "Plants are the energy base for the whole system. A tree is not a tree all by itself. It hosts jillions of creatures—birds, insects, fungi. Botany leads to the universe."[29]

Earle worked in college as intensely as she had previously. She read, she memorized, she took notes, and she collected specimens. She fit right into the lifestyle of the field scientist whose primary goal is to observe, collect, and describe the full range of creatures, animal or plant, in a given region. Cataloguing the many different forms of underwater plant life that she discovered during her dives, she noted their habitats and growing patterns underwater. She would measure significant details about immediate water conditions: depth, current, temperature, light, and salinity. She would take a small sample and bring it into the laboratory. She would write notes on its growing habits and carefully draw it in detail. She would then dry and press it for her growing collection of plant specimens from the Gulf of Mexico.

Earle's skill in drawing plants was recognized by others, who hired her to do botanical illustrations for their research. Combining her scholarship with the money she earned doing this work and other jobs as a laboratory assistant, and with help from her parents as well, Earle had enough money to pay her tuition. She graduated from Florida State in 1955 at the age of 19.

WOMEN CAN BE SCIENTISTS, TOO

Sylvia Earle followed her mentor, Harold Humm, when he moved from Florida State to Duke University. Completing her master's degree in 1956, she had no doubts about continuing on to earn a doctorate. She considered Cornell University, in upstate New York, but decided to stay at Duke and continue studying with Professor Humm. Although she was interested in fulfilling the course requirements for this advanced degree, she was more interested in getting on with the real research, which would culminate in her doctoral dissertation. She already had a good start on a dissertation-quality study: the catalog of underwater plants in the Gulf of Mexico that she had so avidly begun at the Alligator Harbor Marine Lab.

Many graduate students have some financial support from their schools. Instead of getting jobs in restaurants or offices, a lot of graduate students try to get teaching assistantships: jobs within the university that pay them to help professors teach classes, grade papers, and operate research projects. With a teaching assistantship, a graduate student stays focused on learning while earning a small salary.

Considering herself a potential candidate, Sylvia Earle applied for a graduate teaching assistantship. For the first time in her life, she faced discrimination against women. She was smart, she was a hard worker, and she had good grades and an excellent work record. Despite her excellent qualifications, the men in charge at the graduate school believed in giving teaching assistantships to people that they knew would enter the field and become serious scientists. Believing that it was unlikely that a woman would follow that path, they turned down Earle's application.

"They said, 'It has to go to a man, because a woman will just get married and have babies,'" Earle said years later. "Of course I was disappointed, but that attitude wasn't considered unusual in those days." [30]

Ironically, not long after this, Sylvia Earle did leave graduate school to get married and start a family. Never did she intend this decision to mean that she was abandoning her love of science and of the ocean. She had completed most of the required coursework toward the Ph.D. degree, and her major work now was to pass examinations and write a dissertation. She felt, however, that it was time to add a personal dimension to her life, which had been so focused and so alone thus far. "I had been stuffing my brain with books and lab work for as long as I could remember," she said in 1989. "I think I was suffering from information overload. I decided that I wanted to go out and do things that were *real*." [31]

Earle had fallen in love with John Taylor, another graduate student, while studying zoology. They married in 1957, when Sylvia was 21 years old and her new husband was 22. They moved together to her home state of Florida and, for a little while, worked together for the National Park Service. They lived in Live Oak, then in Gainesville, and finally in Dunedin, the little town where Earle's parents still had a home. In 1960, their first child, Elizabeth, was born. Two years later, a son was born. The baby was named John Richie, two family names.

Those were the days, Earle wrote later, when "I began a great balancing act as active scientist, supportive wife, and, in due course, mother to two small children. I was already scrambling to maintain a household while keeping up my long-term research project on the ecology of marine plants in the Gulf of Mexico." [32] Her parents kindly helped by taking care of the two little children, and Earle began commuting to Duke University in Durham, North Carolina, to complete the work for her degree.

Oceanographers tend to be attracted to the sea's animal life, but Earle's mentor in college studied algae, and she caught his enthusiasm. She came to believe that all life began with plants, and she decided to study botany. Not many scientists were in that field at the time, but Earle (pictured here with one of the sub pilots on the *Jim* dive) became a master of it and was praised for her skill at drawing the plants she studied. Some of her most important early work involved observations over time, studying plants not only for what they were but for how they changed.

KEEPING UP WITH THE OCEAN

Back home in Dunedin, Earle could frequently slip into the familiar Gulf waters and observe the plants she was studying. She continued to build her collection of plant specimens. She kept copious notes, chronicling the growth and reproductive patterns of the plants that interested her. She was building a four-dimensional knowledge—not only knowing the plants by diving down to observe, touch, and collect them but also watching them through time, through daily, seasonal, and annual changes.

Along the way, Earle kept up with the news in the field of oceanography. Jacques-Yves Cousteau, collaborating with engineer Jean Mollard, now roamed ocean depths in a newly designed submersible, *Diving Sauce,* a little two-person craft that allowed him to reach 1,000 feet below sea level in 1960.

That same year, French diver Jacques Piccard and U.S. naval officer Don Walsh rode in a bathyscaphe (a type of submersible craft for exploration) called *Trieste* to a depth of 35,800 feet in the Mariana Trench near the Philippines, the deepest known region of the ocean. In 1962, several divers, including Cousteau, experimented with dives that lasted a day or a week. Their underwater bases were atmospherically controlled undersea laboratories from which they forayed repeatedly, essentially living underwater.

Meanwhile in Sarasota, Florida, south of where the Taylors lived, Eugenie Clark was earning the nickname "Shark Lady" with her remarkable work at the Cape Haze Marine Laboratory. In 1953, Clark's book about swimming with the sharks, *Lady with a Spear,* had become a national bestseller. In 1955, she had founded the Cape Haze Marine Laboratory, a private research center where she and fellow field scientists studied the behavior and ecology of fishes not only in the Gulf waters but also around the world.

In 1962, Sylvia Earle was 27 years old, a wife and a mother of two, and still working on a doctoral study of plants in the Gulf of Mexico. She read with excitement and envy about the adventures of people like Jacques Cousteau and Eugenie Clark. She heard the news that the *Williamsburg,* a World War II gunboat converted into a presidential yacht, was being renovated for scientific use. It had been renamed the *Anton Bruun* after a renowned Danish marine biologist. The highly regarded Woods Hole Oceanographic Institution was chartering the ship to participate in a four-year International Indian Ocean Expedition. That year, the 244-foot steel ship embarked on a four-year research cruise through the Indian and Pacific oceans and the Caribbean Sea. Little did Earle know that, thanks to the *Anton Bruun,* she would soon be clocking dive hours as significant to diving history and to marine research as those of her heroes Jacques-Yves Cousteau and Eugenie Clark.

4

Diving into Marine Biology
1964–1969

There I sat, warm and dry, staring into a shimmering, well-behaved circle of blue, rimmed with silver. I poked my finger into the pool, then my toes, then let go, plunging feet first onto soft sand three feet under the sub, 125 feet beneath the ocean's surface.

—Sylvia Earle, about her first lookout dive from a submarine

HEADING TO THE INDIAN OCEAN

A fellow oceanography student, K. M. Aziz, had been slated to travel on *Anton Bruun* for its final research expedition in the Indian Ocean. At the last minute, his plans changed, and Harold Humm suggested that Sylvia Earle go instead. Why her? she wondered.

"They want a marine botanist," Professor Humm responded. She reminded him that she had never been west of the Mississippi River.

"All the more reason why you should go," he answered. "It will be good for you. Just do what you've been doing in the Gulf of Mexico." [33]

She read with wonder the itinerary planned for this last leg of the voyage. They would sail the Indian Ocean, one of the world's major bodies of water, with Africa to the west, Saudi Arabia to the northwest, India and Pakistan to the north, Indonesia to the northeast, and Australia to the east. The expedition would begin in Mombasa, Kenya, on the eastern coast of Africa, and travel toward the Seychelles, a chain of islands topping a massive ocean ridge 750 miles east of the African continent, just south of the equator. The researchers aboard *Anton Bruun* would travel to islands rarely visited and never truly explored since medieval Arab navigators such as Ibn Battuta first charted those waters.[34] They would visit islands dotting the coast of Africa and sail into the Gulf of Aden, toward the Middle East. "I would be among the first to see and document the underwater aspects of most of the reefs and islands visited," Earle realized, "locations that read like a modern adventure-travel agenda with a few extra twists. . . . How could any ocean scientist worth her salt resist?"

Her husband and parents encouraged her. For six weeks, they could take care of the house and children. Her four-year-old daughter, Elizabeth, just made her mother promise to be home for Christmas.

It gave Earle pause, though, when the chief scientist on the expedition, Dr. Edward Chin, asked delicately whether she or her husband minded that Sylvia would be the one and only woman aboard the *Anton Bruun*. Others were of the opinion that she should not go, said Dr. Chin, but he didn't see it as a problem. The more she thought about it, the more Earle realized that in most of her classes and field work projects so far, she had been one of the few women—often the only woman. She had learned to maneuver through those situations:

> I had discovered that most potential hassles never material-
> ized if you minded your business, didn't expect favors or
> try to horn in on male parties or jokes, were prepared to
> do twice as much work for half as much credit—and, of
> paramount importance, kept a well-honed sense of humor.

She signed on; packed up her mask, fins, and snorkel; and headed for the Indian Ocean.

A WOMAN OF THE WORLD

She was the only woman aboard, one of only a few divers on the research team, and a person who had never before traveled outside the United States, and yet all those limitations disappeared from Sylvia Earle's consciousness as she made her first dive off *Anton Bruun* into the Indian Ocean. "Like a child turned loose alone at F.A.O. Schwarz," she wrote, "I wanted to be everywhere at once, peering into the great, soft folds of clownfish anemones, poking at giant sea cucumbers, following pairs of yellow butter-fly fish, standing on my head to get a better look at a spotted eel in an angled crevice, coaxing a tiny octopus from its lair." She would dive for hours every day and then examine, measure, note, and catalog for hours every night. Her journal was filled with entries written in the wee hours of the morning. She would greet the ship's baker as he arose at 3 A.M. to start the ovens to bake the day's bread, while she was still making copious notes on all the things she had observed the day before.

Earle spent much of the mid-1960s on oceanographic expeditions around the world, like this one on *Anton Bruun* in 1964. In 1966 her experience paid off: her mentor, Eugenie Clark, invited her to direct the Cape Haze Marine Laboratory in Sarasota, Florida. In the same year, Earle published her doctoral dissertation on algae in the Gulf of Mexico, and her reputation was made. Earle is pictured above with a bird, known as a Noddy, that crashed into the *Anton Bruun*. She took care of the bird until it could fly again.

Off a tiny island inhabited by crabs, terns, and tropical birds, she discovered a pile of decomposing elephant tusks 15 feet underwater that was home to a watchful grouper. Sea pens, whip corals, and soft corals—one a brilliant indigo blue—fringed a coral reef along the shore of Mouniameri Island in the Comores. The fish seemed as fascinated by Earle as she was by them. Never having been hunted, they innocently swam up, surrounded her, and stared in curiosity. She returned home with her memory and her notebooks full of plants and animals that she had never seen before, feeling that she now belonged in their world.

Over the next two years, from 1964 to 1966, Earle worked several more times aboard *Anton Bruun*. The vessel continued on worldwide research expeditions, cruising around the Cape of Good Hope and across the Atlantic Ocean to the Caribbean then through the Panama Canal to the Pacific coastline of Central and South America. One of the islands it approached was Más a Tierra in the Juan Fernandéz Islands, 300 miles west of Valparaíso and midway down the long Pacific coastline of Chile.

Más a Tierra was popularly known as Isla Robinson Crusoe, because it was near this tiny Pacific Island that Alexander Selkirk, a hotheaded, Scottish-born sailor, quarreled with his captain and was left behind, all alone, in 1704. There he stayed, fending for himself, for four years—a true story that 15 years later inspired Daniel Defoe to write his famous novel *The Life and Adventures of Robinson Crusoe*.

Aboard *Anton Bruun*, Earle visited Más a Tierra in November 1965. No one had ever donned scuba gear to explore the waters surrounding the island. On her second day, diving with ichthyologists (scientists who study fish) at 100 feet, Earle spotted a bright pink plant she had never seen before.

Clusters of upright stalks were crowned with an explosion of sinuous gelatinous branches that rippled with the slightest current. When still, individual plants resembled pink palm trees or umbrellas turned inside out by the wind. She later wrote, "It was unlike anything I had seen before, and subsequent searching proved that it was not just a new species or genus but an entirely new family, perhaps a new order, of red algae."

Having discovered a plant never known before, it was Earle's honor and responsibility to name it. She considered calling it "Seussiform"—only the mother of two toddlers would look at a natural formation and think about a favorite author of children's books! Ultimately, though, she and fellow graduate students combined descriptive English and Latin words with the name of their beloved professor and named the plant *Hummbrella hydra*.

JOINING THE SHARK LADY

Earle came home to Florida, but she didn't stop exploring. Soon after her adventures aboard *Anton Bruun*, Eugenie Clark invited her to visit the Cape Haze Marine Laboratory. Clark had begun developing a plant collection as part of her laboratory, and she asked for Earle's help.

Forty-four-year-old Eugenie Clark provided Earle with a perfect role model. Clark had received a Ph.D. in zoology in 1950 and had participated in oceanographic research in California, the Middle East, and the Philippines. She was married and had four children, who were, in 1966, 14, 12, 10, and 8 years old. Like Earle, Clark believed in diving face-to-face with her subject—and in her case, the subject was sharks. It was not unusual for Clark to swim among sharks, big or small, docile or deadly. Clark learned to maneuver in their waters and study them on their own terms. In the early 1960s, as Earle put it, Eugenie Clark "tucked me under her flipper."[35] In 1965, while Clark was executive director of the Cape Haze Marine Laboratory, Earle became its resident director.

Even with such a strong role model, Earle found it difficult to be a wife, a mother, a scientist, and a professional all at the same time. As she advanced in her career during the early 1960s, her marriage with John Taylor faltered. "I guess it really is no wonder that my marriage eventually came apart," she said years later. "There was a lot of compatibility, but also a lot of differences. Jack is a fine naturalist, and he was quite happy to take on a little green patch in Florida and settle down in the pine trees, and I didn't want to settle down at all. I just wanted to take on the world."[36]

MAKING MORE WAVES

In 1966, Sylvia Earle completed her dissertation, *Phaeophyta of the Eastern Gulf of Mexico*. ("Phaeophyta" means brown algae, which include the plants called kelp.) Most doctoral dissertations gather dust in university library basements, but Earle's was different. Fellow oceanographers recognized that, in a number of ways, she had done something new and important. First of all, Earle's was one of the first ocean plant studies based on deep-sea diving experience. Earlier marine botanists had studied either shallow-water plants or the occasional deepwater alga washed up on a beach or dredged up with a net. Second, because Earle had been working on the study for more than ten years, she had made observations about change over time. Finally, her study was thorough, detailed, and meticulously careful. It was so important that the editors of the scholarly journal *Phycologia*—the publication in which almost all important work on algae was published— devoted an entire issue to it.

Personal decisions sometimes influence professional careers. In Sylvia Earle's case, her second marriage, to Giles Mead, curator of fishes at the Harvard Museum of Comparative Zoology, brought her into a new community of ocean scientists. Earle and Mead, who were married in 1966, shared close professional interests, and the two of them worked on several research expeditions together. Earle's two children joined their Boston household, which sometimes included Mead's three children from his previous marriage. Soon, another child was on the way. "It was a period when I tried to do everything for everybody," Earle later commented.

Earle on an *Anton Bruun* expedition to Panama in 1967, a year after she achieved academic acclaim for her work in the Gulf of Mexico. It was less than year after this trip that the eagerly anticipated *Deep Diver* project became a reality, promising to drastically cut the amount of diving time lost in decompression. Earle's first trip in *Deep Diver* took place in February 1968 and lasted four times as would have been possible before. Decompression was accomplished above the surface.

"It was a great balancing act. But then, it's always been a great balancing act."

A WOMAN JOINS MAN-IN-SEA

In 1968, the oceanographic world was abuzz with news of the Man-in-Sea Project. Since 1962, Jacques-Yves Cousteau had repeated his experiments, developing new ways for human beings to stay underwater longer. Engineer Edwin A. Link, best known as an early inventor of flight simulators for training pilots, wanted to construct a submersible decompression chamber—a vessel that descended to underwater depths with its own controllable internal air pressure system. Individual scuba divers were limited in dive time by the amount of air they could carry in their tanks. A good portion of their time underwater was spent returning slowly to the surface. If decompression could be accomplished in the submarine rather than on the way back up, then more time could be spent working underwater.

Edwin Link partnered with Florida entrepreneur John H. Perry, Jr., and built *Deep Diver.* They called their invention a "lockout" submarine because from it, a diver would exit into the water and move independently, locked out of the submarine during the dive. *Deep Diver,* however, was "more than a sub," as Link wrote in *National Geographic.* His description made it sound effortless:

> It's a system. . . . We park her on the bottom and build up the gas pressure in the divers' compartment until it equals the pressure on the outside; the hatch drops open and out they go. . . . When they get back in, they simply close the hatch to lock the pressure in with them, and come on up. We hoist her aboard and sail away.[37]

In February 1968, Sylvia Earle climbed into the curious-looking submarine called *Deep Diver.* Once more, her decision to dive raised a few eyebrows, this time not just because she was a woman but also because she was nearly five months pregnant. Years later, her daughter Gale, born in July, would explain her love of the ocean by saying, "I can't help it. I was diving from a submarine before I was born."[38]

In *Sea Change,* Earle described the feeling of sitting in *Deep Diver* on board the launch ship with submarine expert Dennison Breese, watching the hatch close over and feeling the crane pick them up inside the bullet-shaped vessel and drop them down into the 100-foot-deep Bahamian waters:

> With a gentle bump we touched down on an open sandy area peppered with small coral-crowned rocks and miniature forests of the plants I had come to see. Denny signaled the pilot that we were ready for action, and compressed air hissed into our chamber. Immediately my ears felt squeezed, and I held my nose and swallowed to relieve the stress on aching cranial canals and sinuses. Once the gauges in the cabin showed the inside pressure matched outside, Breese unlatched the hatch on the floor of the submersible. The door to the ocean opened. Despite my knowledge of the laws of physics, it seemed improbable to me that pressure inside the sub could keep water from rushing in, but there I sat, warm and dry, staring into a shimmering, well-behaved circle of blue, rimmed with silver. I poked my finger into the pool, then my toes, then let go, plunging feet first onto soft sand three feet under the sub, 125 feet beneath the ocean's surface.

Earle roamed the Bahamian seafloor at a depth of 125 feet for an hour and a half—more than four times as long as she would have been able to spend at that depth had she been diving just with scuba gear. At the end of her too-short stay, she rejoined Breese in *Deep Diver*. The hatch closed, the air systems began adjusting the pressure, and the vessel slowly began to rise. Even aboard the launch ship, Earle and Breese remained a full hour inside *Deep Diver*, their submersible decompression chamber, before they were ready to return to Earth's atmosphere.

EVER READY FOR THE NEXT DIVE

Sylvia Earle had just become the first woman scientist to experience a lockout dive from a submarine, but she was not

SATURATION DIVING

When Sylvia Earle and her colleagues live for days or weeks in an underwater habitat, they are practicing "saturation diving." In a number of ways, this practice is different from "bounce diving," the standard sport experience of descending into the water for an hour or so and then carefully coming up again. In saturation diving, divers retreat from the water into atmospherically controlled habitats, like *Tektite, Hydrolab,* or *Aquarius.** Divers in these habitats manage to lead relatively normal lives, but the atmosphere in which they are living is not equivalent to that on Earth. In *Aquarius,* for example, the air stays at a pressure of 2.4 atmospheres. Because of the different air pressure, the divers' voices sound higher in pitch, and they can't whistle.

Divers living in an underwater habitat actually maintain higher-than-ordinary levels of nitrogen in their bodies. Excess nitrogen can cause the bends as bounce divers surface, but saturation divers move smoothly between underwater and habitat without such worries. Excess nitrogen in the bloodstream can also cause "nitrogen narcosis," a state of mind approaching euphoria. Jacques Cousteau once called this condition "antic joy," in which "I struggled to fix my brain on reality."** Nitrogen narcosis can cause a diver to become disoriented. Some keep swimming into the depths, never to surface again.

Saturation divers may experience mild nitrogen narcosis, but because most of them have years of diving experience and work on which they can focus, the risks are not too high. Still, members of a saturation dive team watch out for each other. It may feel like home, but an underwater research habitat is highly complex; team diligence about all life-support systems is essential.

* Information on *Aquarius* and saturation diving comes from William Schane, M.D., "Saturation Diving: It's a Little Different," NAUI report #2520, *The Best of Sources,* Sept./Oct. 1989, NAUI website, *http://www.naui.org/pdffiles/satdive.pdf.*

** Quoted in Earle, *Exploring the Deep Frontier,* p. 105.

resting on her laurels. The wheels in her head were already turning, trying to figure out how she could get back down that deep for that long again.

Back in Cambridge, Giles Mead had noticed an announcement from the Smithsonian that was pinned on a bulletin board at the Museum of Comparative Zoology. It was in reference to Phase II of a project called Tektite, sponsored by the National Aeronautic and Space Administration (NASA). The project was named after tektites, glassy meteorites found on the ocean floor, symbols of the relationship between space and sea exploration. The Navy had recently completed a study of undersea research stations, and now it was partnering with NASA, the Department of the Interior, and other government agencies to develop a saturation diving project. In 1969, four men had lived for two months in a four-room habitat 50 feet underwater in the waters off the U.S. Virgin Islands. After that success, a second phase was planned. Scientists and engineers were invited to submit research proposals for work to be done while living two weeks or more in the "Tektite Hilton."

Earle and her colleagues proposed a collaborative project to study the interaction of fish as they graze on the plants in a circumscribed underwater area. She felt confident about their application. By this point, she had chalked up more hours of research diving experience than most of the marine scientists she knew. She had experience, a reputation, and connections. She just seemed a natural.

Once again, her gender got in the way. The men in charge of Tektite couldn't imagine a woman living and working among men in such close quarters. Fortunately, Tektite project manager James Miller came up with a plan that would win Sylvia Earle her well-deserved time underwater. He proposed that she lead an all-woman Tektite research team. Earle, of course, said yes.

5

The Diver is a Woman
1970–1975

How can you make people care about this vital system, which is filled with forms of life that are as unknown to us as residents of Mars would be?

—Sylvia Earle, on educating
the public about the ocean

DAILY LIFE UNDERWATER

In the summer of 1970, five women moved 50 feet underwater, into the Tektite habitat off the coast of St. John in the U.S. Virgin Islands. They would live near the coral reef fringing Lameshur Bay, inside a national park formed to protect the coral reef. Tektite was a highly engineered, four-chamber, atmosphere-controlled laboratory and living space. It had successfully housed one suite of experiments the year before. Sylvia Earle's all-woman team represented 5 out of a total of 50 scientists scheduled during the seven-month *Tektite II* endeavor.

One goal of the Tektite mission was to determine the feasibility of long-term saturation diving in the service of science. From *Deep Diver*, Earle had been able to exit into the water, move around and explore, and then reenter a dry, breathable atmosphere. *Deep Diver* was analogous to a car that allowed her to drive down into the ocean, get out and walk around, get back in again, and drive back to the surface. In contrast, Tektite was a house that sat on the ocean floor. It had a front door and four rooms, including sleeping, eating, and hygiene facilities. Earle and her crewmates moved underwater with no plans to resurface or return to a boat or to shore for two whole weeks.

It was an odd-looking edifice, this Tektite structure that they called home: a large, rectangular, industrial-looking metal base on which stood two cylindrical structures. Each cylinder contained two chambers, one stacked over the other. A flexible tunnel connected one chamber to the other. The General Electric Company had designed and constructed the structure, and some said it looked like a giant kitchen appliance.

A diver entering Tektite would swim into the portico and then up through the rectangular base to a hatch stairway leading into the right-hand cylinder. The first room entered, dubbed the "wet room," was primarily a laboratory with microscopes and other state-of-the-art scientific equipment. A ladder led to the engine room above, which contained the controls for temperature, air, and freshwater systems. The wet room included a hot shower and clothes dryer; the engine room included a sink, toilet, and food freezer.

From the engine room, a diver could pass through the tunnel into the other cylinder, which contained the living quarters. Upstairs was the control room or "bridge," where the crew's engineer monitored all habitat systems, maintained communication with people above water, and slept on a cot. Below the bridge were quarters for the rest of the crew. They slept in bunks, prepared food in the tiny galley, and ate, read, and wrote at the table in the center of the room. It was tight and spare, but there were some comforts, such as carpet on the floor, stereo music, and television. "The concessions to comfort," Earle came to understand, "proved not to be luxuries but rather were conducive to good performance during prolonged isolation."[39]

Sylvia Earle had already had spent more than 1,000 hours underwater when she embarked on her Tektite adventure. She had used various sorts of diving equipment: mask and snorkel, helmets, scuba gear, and submersibles. "But I had never before had an opportunity to have unlimited time in the sea, day and night, or the prolonged view of an underwater resident," she realized.[40] The scientific benefits of a two-week stay underwater were many. For someone who considered the marine world her second home, it was a thrilling adventure.

TWO WEEKS UNDERWATER

With the coral reef their backyard and the fish their neighbors, Earle and her crewmates—oceanographers Renate True, Alina Szmant, and Ann Hurley, and ocean engineer Margaret Lucas— quickly adapted to their new home. The atmospheric controls inside Tektite meant that they could come and go at ease. For their forays underwater, they preferred to use a "rebreathing" apparatus. Instead of breathing from a tank full of gas, as most scuba divers do, a Tektite diver breathed her own exhalations after the gases had been "scrubbed"—passed through a

Earle was chosen in 1970 to head a mission of the Tektite project. She and four other oceanographers—the first all-female team— would live for two weeks 50 feet beneath the surface. Divers left Tektite to explore whenever they chose, and the information they gathered was crucial to securing government funding for undersea research. Perhaps more important, the mission fired the public's imagination. Earle and her colleagues instantly became national heroes, and Earle began a new phase of her career: helping the public to understand the sea.

chemical filter to remove carbon dioxide and recombined into a breathable formulation. With tanks, a diver's exhalation bubbled into the water, but rebreathers were silent and bubble-free. They made it easier to approach sea creatures without alarming them and to hear the sounds of their world: the grunt of a grouper, the tiny clicks of shrimp swimming by, the crunch as a parrot-fish munched the algae off a chunk of limestone.

With the new equipment, Earle and her companions could explore the water whenever they chose, day or night, as long and as often as they wanted. "To stay inside proved impossible when five tarpon, large silver-scaled fish with luminous eyes, arched and turned right by the window," Earle wrote. "In clear water, even at 70 feet, a bright moon and a sky full of stars gave enough light for us to move freely without bumping into large objects."[41] Diving without lights, the crew put on a light show, their fins kicking up wakes of phosphorescent blue sparkles.

The scientific results of Tektite II were published in two volumes edited by Earle and her colleagues. One volume included ten experimental results on the ecology of coral-reef fishes; the other had eight results on coral-reef invertebrates and plants. Earle contributed a study of marine plants and the fish that eat them, with an annotated list of 154 plant species collected in Lameshur Bay. Twenty-six of those species had never been recorded in the Virgin Islands before. Not only did she identify the plants she found growing on or near the reef, she also observed grazing fish and noted what they chose to eat. Her plant list included the names of fish found to have eaten each species.

"The Tektite program is a step in the direction toward a better understanding of the underwater world," wrote Bruce Collette of the National Marine Fisheries in his conclusion to the Tektite II study results.[42] Although the seven-month venture had cost $1,240,000, it generated masses of information about the coral-reef environment and its inhabitants. Some of it, Collette argued, such as hourly fish observations or on-the-spot observations of the effects of storms on underwater life, could not have been collected in a single short dive. Collette concluded his comments by voicing the opinion of all the scientists who had lived and worked aboard Tektite (including Sylvia Earle):

"Serious consideration should now be given to developing a National Underwater Laboratory."[43]

As earnestly as all the Tektite scientists agreed with that recommendation, not until 1980 did the U.S. government create the National Undersea Research Program (NURP). The program, designed to support underwater laboratory explorations, was given government funding. As a result of the success of the all-woman Tektite project, a new long-term underwater experimental station called Hydro-Lab was launched in the Bahamas in 1971. The crew included women and men working together.[44]

NATIONAL HEROES

For Sylvia Earle, two weeks of daily life underwater was reward enough. Little did she and her crewmates know that all America was watching, ready to congratulate them as soon as they returned to Earth's atmosphere. One year before, astronauts Neil Armstrong and Buzz Aldrin had taken the "first small step for man, the first giant step for mankind" on the moon. The all-woman Tektite crew received almost the same attention. As Earle often indicated, their accomplishments had a few parallels. The modern world had two "final frontiers" yet to explore: deep space and the deep ocean.

To the surprise of the five female scientists, they were considered heroes when they came back above water. They were invited to have lunch with First Lady Patricia Nixon and Secretary of the Interior Walter Hickel at the White House. *Life* and *Redbook* magazines featured the dive, and the manufacturers of Tang, a powdered orange drink, asked her to endorse their product. "I think the biggest shock came in Chicago," Earle told William White of the *New Yorker*. "They gave us a ticker-tape parade, and we rode through the streets in Mayor Daley's open car—it was *fur-lined*— and Mahalia Jackson sang."[45] In 1970, it was news that five women could have so much courage, independence, and dedication to science. The all-woman crew of *Tektite II* won the attention not only of the scientific community but also of the whole nation. "It was Tektite that really turned me around," Earle said almost 20 years later. She explained:

> Suddenly I just found myself propelled onto center stage. . . . There I was, never having addressed crowds, and now there were dozens of radio and television stations carrying my words. . . . And afterward this sort of thing kept happening, and it caused me to think very hard about how I could convey something about the animals and the plants in the ocean—the system which actually dominates our planet, and which had come to mean so much to me—to millions of people, some of whom had never *seen* a fish in its natural habitat. . . . How do you get people interested in that, and how can you make people care about this vital system, which is filled with forms of life that are as unknown to us as residents of Mars would be?[46]

DR. EARLE OR MRS. MUSEUM?

The success of the all-woman Tektite expedition left Sylvia Earle with personal dilemmas. She had gained the admiration and respect of her fellow scientists at university and government laboratories, but for many scientists, writing an article for *Redbook* or holding an interview on television degraded the serious investigative work they were doing. Earle, they believed, should be publishing scholarly articles, not simplifying her discoveries so that millions of Americans could understand them. Earle disagreed. She recognized that for the sake of the precious ocean, she needed to reach as many people as she could, not just other experts.

Her personal life posed dilemmas as well. Her husband, Giles Mead, had accepted a position in Los Angeles, California, as the director of the Museum of Natural History. They had moved a household with six children—Earle's two, Mead's three, and the child they had together—to the West Coast. As the wife of the museum director, much was expected of her: hosting parties, meeting distinguished guests, and attending special events alongside her husband. Those responsibilities conflicted with the increasing opportunities she was finding as a public advocate for the world's oceans.

She traveled frequently, sometimes to dive and sometimes to speak at important public events. In 1971, she joined a diving expedition off the coast of Panama. In 1972, she led a scientific diving team in the Galápagos Islands. That same year, she served as chief scientist in a new saturation diving expedition off the Florida Keys. She represented American Women for International Understanding at a worldwide conference in China. She became chief scientist on the Hydro-Lab project and, in 1975, a leader of a government-sponsored, submarine-based experiment called the Scientific Cooperative Operational Research Expedition, which allowed scientists free movement 250 feet underwater—200 feet deeper than the Tektite project.

But while professional successes grew, so did personal stresses. In the mid-1970s, Sylvia Earle and Giles Mead separated, and Earle moved to Oakland, California, where she and her three children made their new home.

6

Diving Adventures, Human and Otherwise
1975–1980

Increasingly, I had come to realize that I had to speak out about the irreversible damage we are doing to the world we live in.

—Sylvia Earle, on her role
as a conservation advocate

A DIVE INTO THE PAST

In 1975, Sylvia Earle joined underwater photographer Al Giddings in the Truk Islands in the South Pacific, where a 1944 U.S. air attack had sunk a fleet of Japanese ships, including a 436-foot-long aircraft carrier. A World War II wreck site might not seem, at first glance, to harmonize with the sorts of underwater environments of interest to Earle. In fact, it was a remarkable scientific opportunity to explore a vast collection of artificial reefs whose age was known nearly to the hour. Earle and Giddings dived with Kimiuo Aisek, a 48-year-old resident of the islands. Aisek, who had witnessed the air strike when he was 17 and had been diving the wrecks ever since, was the best guide imaginable.

The Truk Islands, a complex of 11 major islands and many smaller ones, is one of Micronesia's many atolls. Located about 1,000 miles north of the eastern end of Papua, New Guinea, and 2,000 miles east of the Philippines, the cluster of islands is fringed by a massive coral reef, which encloses a 40-mile-wide lagoon and keeps the waters inside relatively smooth and calm. Truk was nicknamed the "Gibraltar of the Pacific" during World War II. Its naturally protected harbor was a key passage point in the shipping channel traveled by freighters and aircraft carriers bringing war supplies and equipment from Japan to the South Pacific, where air and sea battles raged from 1941 to 1945.

On assignment for *National Geographic* magazine, Earle and Giddings spent six weeks exploring and recording the diversity of life that had overtaken the 31-year-old wreckage. They first investigated the massive hulk of *Fujikawa Maru,* an aircraft carrier so big that its two masts stuck out of the water even though its keel rested 130 feet on the ocean floor below. Using scuba apparatuses, they stood on the ship's deck and swam through its passageways, marveling at how marine life had overtaken the scene of human death and disaster. They noted the guns still poised in their mountings, heaps of ammunition in the hold. Algae draped the portholes. Fish clustered by the thousands in the carrier's nooks and crannies. "Over the course of 31 years," wrote Earle, "the entire ship had been transformed from a bare metal monument to human tragedy into a richly productive reef of extraordinary beauty." [47]

The awe never wore off, but Earle soon got down to work. As she explained to Aisek, measurements of the wreck's largest coral specimens could provide important information:

> I explained our task to Kimiuo: I want to locate and tag the largest corals we can find. This will give us an idea of the maximum size reached since the ships sank. Dividing a coral's diameter by 31—its maximum age in years— gives us the minimum average yearly growth rate. We'll also mark and measure small corals and return later to see how much they've grown. Once we've established a new starting point, measurements can be made at any time to see how fast—or how slowly—these corals [had] grown.

One specimen of black-coral, genus *Antipathes*, grew 60 feet underwater and stood 15 feet tall—several times the size of any Earle had seen before. "Many of our measurements," she wrote later, "exceeded those for the same kinds of corals elsewhere in the world." [48]

A MEETING WITH A LIONFISH

Al Giddings focused his camera lens on the kaleidoscopic forms and colors underwater. He and Earle spotted a lionfish, lurking in the barrel of a gun on the ship's stern. When swimming, a lionfish is elegant, as its fins fan out in an intricate design. The beauty of lionfish, however, bears a danger. Along their backs, lionfish have spiny dorsal fins with which they can inject a painful, sometimes deadly, poison into the flesh of an attacker.

Giddings wanted to get a photograph of the lionfish in full regalia, so Earle used her gloved hand to coax it out of the hole.

In the mid-1970s, Earle made several trips to the Truk Lagoon in Micronesia, where she documented plant and animal growth on Japanese shipwrecks from World War II. All the ships had sunk on the same known date, so Earle—shown here with her guide in Micronesia, Kimiuo Aisek, in 1975—could estimate the plants' growth rates. She took specimens from some sections and then observed the plants over time to identify patterns. A photograph that Al Giddings took of one of one of the expeditions made the cover of *National Geographic* in 1976.

It moved and then tilted as it positioned itself to strike. Earle coaxed it again, and again it tilted. Earle wrote:

> That was enough for me. I started to withdraw my hand, but the lionfish suddenly tilted once more, this time vigorously, and through my diving glove I felt a sharp jab below the nail of one finger. I'm sure I only imagined a look of self-righteousness on my attacker as it darted away. Removing the glove, I examined my finger and saw a trickle of green—blood, as it appears more than 50 feet below the surface.[49]

What's worse, she and Giddings had stayed so long at 70 feet underwater that they had to allow an hour of decompression before surfacing. "I was in trouble and I knew it," said Earle.[50]

For once in her life, she shut herself off to the sights underwater. "I closed my eyes and could think of nothing but the intense, stabbing agony that was building in my finger." Tears filled her eyes. With an air regulator in her mouth, there was no way she could cry out. By the time she was finally able to surface, her finger had swollen double in size. It felt like it was on fire. Her arm and shoulder throbbed with pain. It took several hours before her hand went back to normal.

EVERY DIVE TELLS MORE

During the Truk Lagoon expedition, Earle catalogued more than 100 species of algae, 15 of which had never been documented in Micronesian waters. She also discovered one tiny red alga no one had ever identified before. She collected several live specimens of shimmering, blue five-inch-long fish, a species that she did not recognize. She gave the live fish to the Steinhart Aquarium in San Francisco, where they were identified as *Ptereleotris heteropterus,* rarely seen and never before displayed in a public aquarium.

Al Giddings created an archive of underwater images so rich that *National Geographic* editors devoted 36 pages of the May 1976 issue to them, with text written in the lively, personal style that Sylvia Earle so comfortably assumed. She cherished every chance she got to share her message about the sea. This was an opportunity to educate millions of readers about how life underwater connects—intimately and importantly, species to species, from lowly algae to ocean celebrities like whitetipped sharks—with the rest of nature and humankind.

Earle carried her message to an important meeting of the World Wildlife Fund in San Francisco that year. As keynote speaker, she had 45 minutes to convey to hundreds of committed conservation leaders the importance of taking care of the ocean. She spoke about the South Pacific island of Palau, a precious coral-reef environment where a proposed port to accommodate supertankers threatened reefs and livelihoods of local people. "I worked very hard to say a lot of things that represented a lifetime of thinking," Earle later said.[51] Her message came through loud and clear—so effectively, in fact, that it helped inspire a movement to favor protection of Palau's reefs over the supertanker port.

Sylvia Earle's career was shifting to include public advocacy combined with scientific exploration. "Increasingly, I had come to realize that I had to speak out about the irreversible damage we are doing to the world we live in."[52]

A YEAR WITH THE WHALES

For years, Sylvia Earle had paid closest attention to the underwater phenomena that most people ignore: bits of algae, growths atop coral structures, streaming seaweeds. As a botanist, she studied plant life, although her ultimate interest was the entire, interconnected world underwater of which plants play an essential part. Her research, developing over more than 20 years, now encompassed the entire ecosystem.

Earle explored the habitats of humpback whales, from warm tropical seas to cool temperate waters in 1977. Working with whale researchers Roger and Katy Payne in Hawaii and Bermuda, Charles and Virginia Jurasz in Alaska, and Al Giddings throughout observations that included Australia, New Zealand, and South Africa, Earle explored the role whales have in the ecology of the world's oceans.

Even Sylvia Earle—now a seasoned diver, with thousands of dive hours and hundreds of expeditions behind her—felt a chill of anticipation as she first slid into the Hawaiian waters among animals 800 times her size. "Humpbacks have a reputation for being gentle," she wrote of that first dive, "but 40 tons is 40 tons."[53] One whale swooped by her, turning its massive head and eyeing her directly. She gasped—as well as a scuba

This photograph of Earle with her brother Skip and her children Elizabeth, Richie, and Gale was taken aboard the research vessel *Eagle* in 1976. Like *Anton Bruun*, *Eagle* had served the military; it was a former minesweeper that Earle and Al Giddings had converted to a film platform. This period marked a turning point for Earle: she had been moving toward public education and environmental protection ever since Tektite, but it was in 1977, her "year with the whales," that she really began to take control of her career.

diver can gasp—as a different creature headed straight for Al Giddings and then artfully lifted its flipper, missing him by inches. "I stopped worrying then," said Earle.[54] The whales were curious, coordinated—and not aggressive.

For weeks, Earle and the Paynes, along with graduate students, photographers, and their assistants, spent hours underwater, interacting with the whales. Lahaina, the port of Maui, was renowned for its whale population. Hundreds of humpbacks could be seen in water nearby as early as November and as late as May. It was known that the whales gave birth to their young during those winter months, but many questions remained unanswered. Little of the information already known about whales came from direct observation underwater.

LEARNING MORE ABOUT THE WHALES

The Paynes focused their research questions on the humpbacks' songs, wanting to know more about how and why they made the eerie, held-out notes and tone cycles, which were so loud that divers could feel the sound vibrate through their bodies. Sylvia Earle focused her observations on the interdependence of whales with other living organisms, plants and animals. She saw a whale as a huge moving island, an environmental substrate on which other life depends. She already knew that a whale's hide, like a ship's hull, was home for a variety of barnacles, algae, and parasites, and she was determined to observe just which plants and animals clung to the whales and how their life cycles interacted with that of their giant hosts.

Once the whales left their winter home, Earle headed north as well. Many scientists suspected that the same whales swam from Hawaii to Alaska each year, but in 1977, no one had proven that hypothesis. In Glacier Bay, Earle and Giddings moved aboard *Ginjur,* the home and lab of the Jurasz family. Not only Chuck and Virginia but also their children, Peter, 10, and Susan, 16, focused intently on observing and recording whale appearances and habits. They knew individual whales so well that they had named them. Dot-Dash had a marking on one fin that looked like an upside-down exclamation point. Garf was the one baby humpback in the bay that summer, always side by side with her mother, Gertrude.

Significant findings came out of the months that Earle, the Paynes, the Juraszes, and their assistants spent living with the humpback whales. The Paynes continued their research on how whale songs evolve from year to year. All neighboring humpbacks sing a similar song one year; returning the next year, they begin with that song, but it soon metamorphoses into a new rendition. The Juraszes confirmed and documented with Al Giddings their observations that humpbacks trap krill, tiny shrimplike crustaceans, by generating "bubble nets." A whale blows a ring of bubbles that corrals the krill and keeps them from swimming away. Then the whale shoots up in the middle of the cluster, mouth wide open, hungry for krill. The Juraszes also moved closer to confirming their hypothesis that whales migrate routinely between Alaska and Hawaii.

Earle identified the community of barnacles most likely to adhere to humpback fins and tails. She found, for example, two layers of barnacles on some tail flukes: acorn barnacles, on top of which grew goose barnacles. She and Al Giddings created a documentary film called *Gentle Giants of the Pacific* for the National Geographic Society. Through Earle's diplomatic efforts, serving as ambassador from the sea, the film was broadcast not only on American television but in nations around the world. Earle personally showed the film in many countries, including the Soviet Union, Hong Kong, and China.

LIFE LESSONS LEARNED UNDERWATER

Looking back, Sylvia Earle recognized that her year with the whales marked a significant point in her own evolution. For one thing, she had pushed her capabilities as an underwater scientist to new limits. "My 'year of the whales,' 1977, took me to the edge of where I could go as a free-swimming diver," she wrote in her book *Sea Change*. Diving with these huge, intelligent, interactive animals sharpened her awareness that knowledge of the world underwater can be enhanced by adopting the point of view of those who live there. By swimming among whales, she could "vicariously glimps[e] deeper realms through the eyes of the whales."[55]

More subtly, Earle recognized that in embarking on her year with the whales, she was taking more responsibility for shaping her own work future. With the Paynes and Giddings, she had sought and obtained funding from the National Geographic Society, the World Wildlife Fund, the California Academy of Sciences, the New York Zoological Society, and Hawaii's Lahaina Restoration Foundation—and without their support, the year of whale work could not have happened.

"That was the first time—aside from my research on seaweeds—that I had consciously said, 'This is something I want to do, and I'll go out and find financial support, and *do* it,'" she said in an interview more than ten years later. "Up to then, I realized, most of what I had been doing—in terms of expeditions and so on—had been *reacting* to opportunities." At the age of 42, "I was beginning to take control of my own life."[56]

7

The Better to See the World Underwater

1980–1985

A NEW DIRECTION

By 1978, Sylvia Earle had experienced just about every sort of technology that had been developed to allow human beings to spend time underwater. As a teenager, she had worn a diving helmet. As a college student, she had learned to scuba dive. She had driven in small submarines. She had lived in and dived from long-term underwater habitats. She knew the dangers, the risks, the challenges, and the rewards. She could also see ways in which things could be done better, for the sake of comfort and of scientific investigation. Earle dedicated the next few years of her life to advancing the technology of undersea exploration.

Her new path began with her October 1979 underwater walk with *Jim,* the atmosphere-controlled diving suit that allowed her to make the deepest dive anyone had made without a tether to the surface. The dive was monitored by Graham Hawkes, a British engineer who had recently modified the diving suit and now sat aboard a control ship, 1,250 feet above Earle and *Jim.* Thus far, *Jim* had been used primarily in industry, especially by workers installing and repairing deep-sea oilrigs. Hawkes was pleased to see *Jim* being used in the service of science.

A BOOK FOR ALL READERS

That year, Sylvia Earle was working on a book, together with Al Giddings and the staff of the National Geographic Society. She had published many scientific papers, the collection of Tektite reports, and five articles for *National Geographic* magazine, but this would be the first book Earle had created for the general reading public. It was an ambitious endeavor: a large-format, full-color, 300-page book devoted to the history of underwater exploration. One of Earle's most admired heroes, Jacques-Yves Cousteau, agreed to write the introduction, and his plea for worldwide awareness set the tone of the entire book. "While decision-makers hesitate and living ocean resources dwindle," wrote Cousteau, "the public is awakening to the existence of sea resources and to the man-made dangers that threaten them . . . the very survival of the human species depends upon the maintenance of an ocean clean and alive, spreading all around the world." [57]

Exploring the Deep Frontier was published in 1980, at just about the same time that news was spreading of the 1,250-feet-deep untethered walk Earle took in *Jim*. Sharing their triumphs, Sylvia Earle and Graham Hawkes reconnected in Washington, D.C., during celebrations for the publication of Earle's new book. Sparks flew between them as they discussed the future of untethered research diving equipment. Earle ticked off the features she needed. The process was like taking a fish aquarium and turning it inside out. Earle explained:

> . . . a one-person system that I could wear like a comfort-able suit of clothes, with which I could travel freely (no tether!) from the ocean's surface to the greatest depths 35,800 feet down, and that had arms and hands that could be used to touch, feel, and effectively retrieve objects encountered. I also thought it would be nice to be able to stay for more than a few hours—or come back quickly, if I wanted to. [58]

Hawkes started scribbling, and he came up with the idea of a "bubble sub," a clear, spherical submarine, within which one person could stay for many hours—easy enough to operate that the same person could both pilot and explore. Earle and Hawkes agreed that they would work together to build, test, and market the dream machine. They founded a pair of companies, Deep Ocean Technology and Deep Ocean Engineering, and set up shop in Sylvia Earle's Oakland, California, garage.

Deep Ocean Technology's first machine, *Rig Rover*, was a robotic device designed to service offshore oil rigs—and raise the capital needed to build the company. Deep Ocean

In the later 1980s, Earle played a more active role in directing the two design companies she had founded with Graham Hawkes. Deep Ocean Engineering produced this vehicle, *Phantom*, in 1985. The portable, video-equipped *Phantom* has since found numerous applications in the military, in research, and in entertainment. This photograph of Earle and *Phantom* in San Francisco dates from 1988.

Engineering focused first on the design and development of *Deep Rover*, a one-person submarine that resembled Hawkes' vision of a "bubble sub." The prototype sub was built in conjunction with Phil Nuytten's company, Can Dive, and used for solo dives. Earle holds the women's world record for diving *Deep Rover* to 3,300 feet.

PERFECTING THEIR BUSINESS APPROACH

Deep Ocean Engineering needed investors in order to develop the engineering concepts, and they tried many different avenues. One learning moment came during a meeting with a top executive from the oil company Chevron. To demonstrate how well *Rig Rover*'s mechanical arms worked, Hawkes used them to draw an intricate undersea creature. The Chevron executive harumphed, "When we need to draw shrimp underwater, we'll give you a call." [59] They shifted their business strategy, renamed the machine *Bandit*, and started emphasizing how well it could screw, clamp, and lift oilrig parts underwater. Shell Oil was the first to purchase and put a *Bandit* model into operation. Nine more were sold for oilrig building and repair operations in the next few years.

Like all gifted inventors, Hawkes did not let his imagination rest with *Bandit*. In 1985, Deep Ocean Engineering produced *Phantom*, a small, portable, remotely operated underwater vehicle. Equipped with a standard video camera as part of its operating apparatus, *Phantom* spirited its way into all sorts of situations—not only at work on the underwater portions of ocean oilrigs but also at Disneyworld, various military operations, and numerous research projects.

ALVIN, THE CELEBRITY SUBMARINE

Called by Sylvia Earle "the durable workhorse of research submersibles,"* *Alvin* has been assisting research divers for four decades. He makes his home at the Woods Hole Oceanographic Institution, the nation's premier underwater research center, located just north of Martha's Vineyard in Massachusetts.

Alvin is shaped like a baby submarine and is 23 feet long and 12 feet tall. He has a pointed nose, a blunt rear end, and a little pilothouse on top. Usually three people, a pilot and two scientists, travel inside. They can peer out tiny portholes or get a broader view through video cameras mounted outside. Manipulator arms and a basket attached to *Alvin*'s bow provide tools to collect scientific samples.

The vessel *Alvin* first dipped into Massachusetts waters on June 5, 1964. Soon, shipped to the Bahamas, a remotely operated *Alvin* was plunging to a depth of 7,500 feet. Piloted by two scientists, the submersible reached a depth of 6,000 feet. Since then, *Alvin* has been working hard, primarily on

NEW SUBMERSIBLES AT WORK AND PLAY

Sylvia Earle had already befriended sea lovers at Disneyworld. In 1982, as the Florida-based, futuristic Disney venture Epcot Center was in the planning stages, she joined other ocean experts to advise on the creation of the "Living Seas Pavilion." The Disney staff wanted to create a vision of the world underwater in the twenty-first century. Earle participated in invigorating conversations with Kym Murphy, the Living Seas project director; William Nierenberg, the director of San Diego's Scripps Institution of Oceanography; and Robert Ballard, the intrepid undersea explorer who later became famous for exploring the wreck of the *Titanic* with *Alvin,* the robot-submarine. Those conversations contributed to the shape of

geological expeditions. He has been a stalwart member of research teams on the Mid-Atlantic Ridge, the Cayman Trough, the Galápagos Rift, Bermuda, Hawaii, and the West Coast of North America, from Oregon to Acapulco.

Alvin's best-known expedition was the 1986 exploration of the wreck of the U.S.S. *Titanic.* On September 1, 1985, a team of French and American explorers, using primarily unmanned submersibles and video technology, first spotted the remains of the luxurious ocean liner that struck an iceberg and sank in frigid Atlantic waters in 1912, 450 miles northeast of Newfoundland. The wreck lay 12,468 feet— two and a half miles—underwater.

To explore and photograph the grand ship's rooms and passageways, American explorer Robert Ballard returned to the site the next summer. For this mission, he used *J.J.*, a 28-inch-long unmanned submersible, and *Alvin*, with three men aboard.

* Earle, *Sea Change,* p. 51.

the Living Seas Pavilion at the Epcot Center: a 6-million-gallon aquarium, the largest saltwater environment ever built.

Now, hearing of *Phantom* in 1985, Kym Murphy decided to incorporate Earle and Hawkes's new dream machine into the Living Seas Pavilion. A *Phantom* submarine was submerged so that its video camera viewed the world from inside the aquarium. Images were transmitted onto a screen that greeted visitors as they arrived. As a family stepped into the Living Seas Pavilion, they instantly got a glimpse of themselves and other human visitors from the point of view of the creatures living in the water. Thus *Phantom* took center stage in this popular display of the future of the world underwater.

While *Phantom* was a hit at Disneyworld's Epcot Center, Hawkes and Earle's versatile submersible went to work all over the world. Helicopters could lift one of the vehicles and carry it to a hard-to-reach area. Naval and police forces used both manned and remotely controlled *Phantoms* to explore underwater accident and crime sites, search for unexploded mines, and perform hull inspections. Remotely controlled *Phantom* subs roamed under the ice of Antarctica, helping scientists explore dry valley lakes near McMurdo Sound. Meanwhile, Graham Hawkes and his engineering team developed *Deep Flight*, the equivalent of a one-person underwater airplane, designed to dive to more than 1,000 feet and travel more than 10 miles per hour.

Earle left Deep Ocean Engineering to accept an appointment as Chief Scientist for NOAA (National Oceanic and Atmospheric Administration) in Washington, D.C., in 1990. Hawkes went on to form his own company to develop *Deep Flight*. The assets of Deep Ocean Engineering were sold to a commercial diving company in 2000.

Two years after Earle left Deep Ocean Engineering, in 1992, she founded DOER (Deep Ocean Engineering and Research), a company that builds advanced subsea robotics and submersible systems. DOER has developed a wide range of application-specific remotely operated systems for underwater and subterranean environments, in addition to their own Ocean Explorer ROV series. DOER works closely with Phil Nuytten's Nuytco Research, providing operational support and training for *Deep Worker* and *Deep Rover* submersibles and advanced one atmosphere systems such as a one-man underwater diving suit called *Exosuit*. Earle is chairman of DOER, while her daughter Elizabeth Taylor runs the day-to-day operations of the company with her husband.

A VISIT TO THE EARLE HOUSEHOLD

In the spring of 1988, William White, a writer for *New Yorker* magazine, visited Sylvia Earle at home. Earle was 53 years old. She had lived at the same Oakland, California, address for a dozen years. Two of her children, now adults, lived on the property, and her youngest daughter, Gale, was attending college. Also part of the household was her husband, Graham Hawkes. Two years earlier, in 1986, he and Sylvia Earle had become partners in marriage as well as in business. Hawkes's four children often visited, too.

Earle's son Richie and her eldest daughter, Elizabeth, worked with Deep Ocean Engineering. Elizabeth had also become a lead volunteer at San Francisco's Steinhart Aquarium. She worked with a wide range of animals, from electric eels, octopi, and manatees to many kinds of reptiles and amphibians. She adopted some of the animals that were unsuitable for display at the aquarium and provided temporary housing or breeding programs for others.

With animals added in, the household population rose significantly. According to White, the resident pets included "two dogs, six cats, a parrot, a macaw, two geese, an iguana, an East African horned chameleon, several snakes, some fish, some tarantulas, a caiman, and an alligator." Named Charlie, the alligator would accept a fish offered by human hands.[60]

Large expanses of the house and grounds were devoted to

Sylvia Earle and Graham Hawkes were married in 1986, and the household they shared became home to family, business, and a menagerie
of exotic pets. Sylvia's daughter Elizabeth holds "the infamous Charlie
the Alligator," whom Elizabeth adopted while working at the Steinhart
Aquarium in San Francisco, while Graham Hawkes looks on in this
family photo.

the company, which employed 20 people beyond the corps of
family members. One room of the house served as a marine
biology laboratory for Earle. This was where she kept her
ever-growing collection of algae and other underwater plant

specimens. Between the house and the test pool, Hawkes had built a studio, with south-facing glass walls and numerous drafting tables for him and his engineering and design team. The pool served for both business and pleasure. Many a new component or vehicle was first put to the test in it. Theirs was a house full of energy, activity, and enthusiasm—dedicated to the endless exploration of the natural world, both above and below water, and charged with the same love of learning that had characterized Sylvia Earle since early childhood.

8

America's Sturgeon General

1985–1992

GROWING CONCERN FOR THE ENVIRONMENT

Deep Ocean Engineering had become a successful business, but Sylvia Earle was drawn to opportunities to influence national ocean policy. Concern was rising around the world about Earth's environment and the damage human beings were causing to it. What had long looked like progress on so many fronts—industrial, agricultural, manufacturing—was taking a toll on the health of the Earth's land, air, and sea. Over the course of the 1970s and into the 1980s, people determined to correct the human course of technology in order to save Earth's future were making their voices heard and were forming organizations devoted to this cause.

Earle could see the damage first hand. When she went back to her beloved west coast of Florida and swam in the Gulf of Mexico, the water was murky. The town of Clearwater no longer deserved the name. It was, Earle told William White of the *New Yorker,* "constantly turbid from all the dredging activity, the industrial pollution and agricultural run-off and other chemicals that flow into the Gulf."[61] Pollution was affecting water quality around the world and threatening whole populations of underwater plants and animals.

Meanwhile, debris was mounting on beaches and seafloors. It was a longstanding practice among naval and merchant ships—and, indeed, in many of the nation's cities— to dump trash into the ocean. In centuries past, when things were made of hemp, wood, paper, and cotton—even corrodible metals—the trash decomposed in the waves and saltwater. In Earle's lifetime, since the 1940s, petroleum-based plastics had become the materials of choice for everything from toothbrushes to building materials, soda bottles to furniture, fishing line to inflatable dinghies. These were now cluttering Earle's beloved oceans. Finding a Styrofoam cup on Florida's muddy coastal seafloor, Earle meditated on its longevity:

Thoughtfully, I disengaged a starkly barren polystyrene cup (projected lifetime, five hundred years) from where it languished in folds of soft gray-brown mud. Had a cup such as this been tossed overboard five centuries before, when Christopher Columbus was making his way across the Atlantic, it might still be around. It occurred to me that beachcombers five centuries hence might find this very one, but I decided to interfere with history and packed it home.[62]

Multiply that cup by hundreds of thousands daily and you get a better sense of what was happening to the world's oceans. The Center for Marine Conservation reported that, as of 1988, the world's fleet of merchant vessels were dumping nearly half a million plastic objects overboard every day.[63] Meanwhile, from smaller boats—both pleasure and commercial fishing vessels—plastic line, nets, lures, and bobbers were being cast into the sea. In 1988, volunteers in Florida coastal waters unwound more than 300 miles of plastic fishing line from a single reef area in a matter of three hours.[64] Plants and creatures were being hooked, snagged, bound, and strangled. Other wildlife, mistaking the floating plastic for food, tried to swallow it. "Death by debris" was a serious threat of growing concern to all who knew and loved the life in the ocean.

DIVING CRATER LAKE

It was beginning to appear that no human enterprise was without its counter-effect on the environment. In Oregon, for example, a power company had tapped into hot springs flowing up out of the earth and was using the natural heat and mechanical energy of the water to generate electricity. The operation was near Crater Lake National Park, a spectacular site in southwestern Oregon. Crater Lake was one of the first areas to be designated a national park, signed into law in 1902 by President Theodore Roosevelt. At its center is a deep lake created by the eruption and collapse of a mountain that local Native Americans called Mazama. Near the lake stands Mount Scott, at a height of 8,929 feet.

When drilling began in the area, environmentalists worried that it would affect the lake. Because springs, streams, lakes, and rivers share the same water table deep underground, they reasoned, manipulations at one point in the system could ripple through, causing unexpected results at other points.

Investigating such a hypothesis is not simple. Observations and measurements recorded over time must verify changes in water quality or temperature. An important place to search for such changes would be deep underwater vents, outlets where water and gases from deeper in the earth's crust exit into the lake itself. If scientists could determine the presence, location, and character of such vents, they could more accurately monitor environmental change.

Enter Sylvia Earle and *Deep Rover*. In August 1988, Earle joined a team intent on creating a baseline map and biological inventory of the floor of Crater Lake. The lake was 1,972 feet at its deepest point. Despite the intense clarity of its water, at that depth, the surroundings would be nearly pitch black, but with all its manipulators and sensors, *Deep Rover* was primed to make the most out of a dive to the bottom.

"At a glance, Deep Rover suggests something out of 'Star Trek,'" wrote William White, who witnessed Sylvia Earle's first Crater Lake descent that summer—the first-ever manned (or "womanned") exploration of the lake bottom. "Its main element is a transparent sphere five feet in diameter, which— iridescent in the sunlight—looked about as insubstantial as a soap bubble, but which is made of acrylic plastic five inches thick," he wrote.[65]

The explorer sits inside the atmosphere-controlled sphere, which is attached to an aluminum frame and fitted out with batteries and other mechanical equipment, including multidirectional thrusters that make the vehicle move. Six-feet-long manipulators reach out on either side, and the diver inside the sphere can observe and operate other observational equipment such as cameras, a depth gauge, lights, sonar, and a gyrocompass. Depending on *Deep Rover*'s position, either voice transmissions or simple electronic pings convey to people on the surface what is going on below.

As she traveled 1,000 feet under and deeper, Earle described what she saw. "There are rocks here, still covered heavily with what looks like snow," she reported. "There are *things* growing on rocks at eleven hundred feet," she soon added. "A vertical face—I found something that looks like moss," she said excitedly.[66] Then, for a moment, her voice disappeared, and all observers had to go on was an occasional ping from the depths of Crater Lake.

Earle's dive was the first step of many accomplished during the three-week study of the lake. The moss she collected had never been observed in freshwater as deep, so it was a scientific milestone. Later dives by scientists from Oregon State University confirmed the presence of warm water and large bacterial mats on the bottom of the lake. Most importantly, perhaps, the projected created public awareness that helped maintain protection for the park. Botanist Sylvia Earle had adopted a greater mission: to protect as well as to explore Earth's watery environment.

THE EXXON *VALDEZ* CATASTROPHE

On March 24, 1989, an accident so disastrous occurred that it shocked the world into reconsidering the preciousness of the ocean. The oil tanker *Valdez,* carrying millions of gallons of crude oil for its parent company, Exxon, ran aground on Bligh Reef in Prince William Sound, Alaska. Punctured and hung up on the reef, the supertanker leaked 11 million gallons of black crude oil into the waters along the Kenai Peninsula, less than 100 miles from the city of Anchorage. Oil dispersed through the waters and spread onto the shore. Three thousand square

By the time of her experience in Crater Lake, Earle had become concerned about the effects of pollution on the natural world. But the *Valdez* disaster in March 1989 changed everything: 11 million gallons of crude oil choked three thousand square miles of ocean and 800 miles of coastline. Earle investigated the site in April with the National Oceanic and Atmospheric Agency (NOAA) and the Coast Guard, and she realized that human behavior could cause environmental damage that no human effort could repair. The Persian Gulf spill followed three years later.

miles of ocean were affected; 800 miles of coastline were saturated with thick, black, unprocessed oil. Thousands of birds and hundreds of sea otters died immediately. The longer-term effects were hard to calculate or imagine.

Three weeks after the *Valdez* foundered, Sylvia Earle and Chuck Jurasz, who had studied whales together 12 years before, visited the besieged waters. They helicoptered over the area, noting the configurations the spilled oil had taken: iridescent slicks on top of the water, strands of earth-red foam bobbing in the waves, and long swaths of black gunk covering the rock-strewn beaches. They went ashore at one spot where life seemed to have survived the spill. Tidal pools glistened with new herring roe. A few sea otters and harbor seals swam offshore. Gulls dipped and squawked above their heads, and they counted three eagles passing by. "That's a good sign, but they're certainly not out of danger," said Earle.[67] She and Jurasz took samples of the herring eggs, along with bits of algae.

On other beaches, the answer was more obvious. Mummy Bay was thick with black residue. Visiting the site with officials of the U.S. government, including the heads of the Coast Guard and the National Oceanic and Atmospheric Agency (NOAA), Earle lifted an oil-slicked rock, revealing dead crabs and mollusks underneath. The scientist in her struggled with the lover of the sea. "It was easy to maintain some detachment while contemplating the theoretical consequences of toxic substances in complex food chains, or while leafing through pages of statistics about the number of dead birds, fish, otters, and other creatures found," she wrote.[68] Nevertheless, the windrows of dead krill and belly-up starfish, the cries of suffering seabirds, and the pitiful gaze of dying otters made the Exxon *Valdez* disaster a personal tragedy for Sylvia Earle.

Although Coast Guard, NOAA, and Exxon officials were on the site immediately, Earle was discouraged at how ill prepared the oil companies as well as U.S. government agencies were to handle the crisis. As long ago as 1972, when U.S.

concerns built the oil pipeline through the Alaska wilderness and out the port of Valdez, Department of Interior staff members had predicted that the major risk would be the reef-lined channel that tankers had to travel as they approached the harbor. Despite forewarning, response strategies had to be made up on the spot. Some clean-up efforts turned out to add further insult to the oil spill's devastating injuries. Under orders given directly by President George Bush, Coast Guard Commandant Paul Yost came to clean up the beaches—but there are some things that human beings, despite hard work, good intentions, and millions of dollars, just cannot do.

"No matter how much money is spent, natural forces—elements that money can *protect* but cannot *buy*—are fundamental for restoration," wrote Sylvia Earle in *Sea Change*, looking back upon the lessons she learned by living through the *Valdez* clean-up efforts. "Not a penny of the $3 billion [ultimately spent by Exxon] brought twice daily tides of clean, fresh water from the surrounding Pacific Ocean, or paid for new larval fish, plankton, otters, birds, or whales."[69]

The catastrophe had only one positive outcome: It heightened corporate, government, and public awareness of the fragile and essential ocean, which so many had been taking for granted for so long.

WORKING WITHIN THE SYSTEM

Time and again, it had come to Sylvia Earle's attention that, in the eyes of the American public and its representatives, the deep frontier of the ocean was not as important as the vast frontier of outer space. She thought of how much publicity and fanfare were given to astronauts while ocean explorers were typically ignored. The government supported NASA, the National Aeronautic and Space Administration—an entire agency devoted to outer-space exploration—but no such independent agency existed to advance the science and technology of inner-space exploration. "There is no underwater equivalent of NASA,"

Earle told the *New Yorker*'s William White in 1989, "and there never has been."[70] It had frustrated her as an entrepreneur seeking support to develop new underwater technologies. It now frustrated her even more deeply as she noted the absence of a well-planned, rational, and scientific approach to the *Valdez* disaster.

Concerns such as these must have been at the forefront of Earle's mind when, in the summer of 1990, President George Bush appointed her chief scientist for National Oceanic and Atmospheric Administration (NOAA). Of all the government agencies, NOAA comes closest to being the nation's "ocean agency," but it is a part of the U.S. Department of Commerce, and includes responsibility for the National Weather Service, National Marine Fisheries Service, the national environmental satellites, ocean and atmospheric research labs, and the National Ocean Service. In recent years, NOAA adopted a more research-oriented mission, supporting the work of the Environmental Protection Agency. Its budget provided for ambitious projects to map the sea from satellites but little to explore it underwater. It also administered a National Underwater Research Program (NURP), budgeted at less than $20 million in congressional funding. The National Marine Fisheries Service (NMFS), also operated by NOAA, worked on behalf of the nation's commercial fishing industry. The appointment of Sylvia Earle represented a new approach to the oceans—marked more by exploration and care than by efforts to exploit. Eager to make a difference, Earle was confirmed by the Senate as NOAA's chief scientist in October 1990.

THE OCEAN IN THE BALANCE

The post gave Earle remarkable opportunities. She joined two other scientists in the Japanese research submarine *Shinkai 6500*, descending in the Nankai Trough off Japan to 13,065 feet—two and a half miles—underwater, another diving first. Earle and fellow scientists marveled at the creatures living in such dimly lit depths, rarely if ever observed by human eyes. They took measurements and collected samples of mud and water for an investigation of biotechnology applications of deep-sea life forms, supported by the government of Japan.

The post gave her ponderous responsibilities as well. It was a time of intense debate and increased concern about the environment, and now Earle entered those conversations as a spokeswoman for the United States of America. Ecologists were voicing their concerns about global warming. Instead of viewing the environment locally, or even nationally, scientists were urging all citizens to recognize that the planet as a whole shared in the consequences of human civilization. Technological advances seemed to have a negative impact on Earth, often thousands of miles from an initial pollution site. Some hypothesized global and irreversible changes. The level of concern was rising about environmental effects such as global warming and also about the ways in which human overpopulation, greed, and commerce were robbing the planet in all its abundance.

Nations around the world debated the fate of the world's sea creatures, not only those caught for food but also the accidental victims of that harvest. Sea turtles were swimming into shrimping nets off the Gulf of Mexico and losing their lives. Salmon were decreasing in number, the essential upstream leg of their life cycle made impossible by hydroelectric dams built across the powerful rivers of the Northwest. Worldwide populations of bluefin tuna had dropped dramatically in just the past two decades. Government agencies attempted to set rules and limits, but commercial fisheries continued to haul in millions of tons of ocean life. The figures were daunting. By mid-century, 20 million tons of seafood had been gathered annually around the world. By 1989, the world catch totaled 86 million tons. Now fishing boats traveled far from home and used highly sophisticated technologies to locate and seize the fish in volume, along with any other sea creatures that happened to be in the same part of the ocean.[71]

Earle was appointed as NOAA's chief scientist in October 1990. In the past, the government had funded oceanic exploration mainly to find ways of exploiting the ocean's resources. Earle's appointment marked a shift in the NOAA's mission: she worked to align the agency more with NASA and to bring research to the forefront. But speaking for the government became more of a burden than she had anticipated, and Earle left the position early in 1992 to become more active in environmental causes.

OIL SPILL IN THE PERSIAN GULF

Meanwhile, war in the Middle East resulted in another massive oil spill. Believing that Iraqi leader Saddam Hussein intended to seize Kuwait and its rich oil fields, American military forces launched Desert Storm in January 1991, forcing Iraqi troops back into their own territory. In retaliation, retreating Iraqi soldiers set fire to 800 oil wells and dumped 12 million barrels of oil on Kuwaiti land and into the Persian Gulf. [72] Once again, the world witnessed miles of blackened beaches and hundreds of thousands of sea plants and animals destroyed. This time, however, the disaster was brought about by the willful acts of human beings.

Sylvia Earle immediately went to the scene. The combination of spilled and burning oil created a disaster that was even worse than the *Valdez* accident. "The first trip was a shattering experience," Earle told a *New York Times Magazine* reporter later that year:

> We traveled out of Kuwait City in buses, looking at this stark landscape with plumes of fire and smoke all around us. We could feel the searing heat. Just searing. And the smoke everywhere billowing up into this immense black cloud. When the wind blows toward the city it becomes unbearable—we had to wear surgical masks.[73]

Traveling down the Saudi Arabian coastline, the visitors witnessed miles of devastation. Oil residues coated the beach and infiltrated the shallow gulf waters. "It's hard to imagine how the turtles will dig through the asphalt on shore to deposit their eggs," Earle told the *New York Times* reporter. She ticked off just a few of the species affected: octopi, squid, corals, migrating birds, and the region's famous pearl oysters. "Nobody knows the impact of oil on that incredible assemblage of plants and wildlife." Her only hope was that, with such ecological horrors publicized around the world, the public would be shocked into vigilance. She told the reporter, "We're still taking for granted these assets that are certainly not free: clean air, water, a habitable environment. Only if we learn from the devastation taking place in a situation like the one in Kuwait will we have a chance not to lose these great assets."[74]

As the world learned of the environmental traumas resulting from the Gulf War, Earle was making public the longer-term environmental results of the Exxon *Valdez* oil spill. Together with John H. Robinson, director of NOAA's hazardous materials program, she held a press conference in April 1991, revealing research results culled from 58 different studies. All told, they showed damage even worse than predicted in the days following the accident. "U.S. Says Harm from Valdez Spill Is Much Worse Than Was Thought," read front-page headlines in the *New York Times* on April 10, 1991. "In the most comprehensive public account of the damage," the article began, "the Government said today that far more wildlife had been killed and that environmental damage would persist much longer than scientists had originally thought." Particularly troubling was the news that the beaches cleaned with the technique of spraying hot seawater did not recover as quickly as those that were left alone.[75]

PRIVATE CITIZEN EARLE

Sylvia Earle must have done considerable soul-searching during the fall of 1991. She announced on January 18, 1992, that she was resigning her post as chief scientist at NOAA. She chose an interesting place to make the announcement: in Houston, at the annual national meeting of the Diving Equipment Manufacturers Association. Her message to the audience was, in essence, that she was returning to her role as a deep-sea diver and advocate of the ocean. "As private citizen Earle, I will be able to do and say things that are not appropriate for a senior official of the United States Government," she announced. "I will be able to actively seek, not just to advocate, a healthy and sustainable marine environment."[76]

Those who knew her told reporters that Earle had felt frustrated while working within the government infrastructure to try to inspire a greater dedication to the world's oceans. One friend later said he was surprised that officials had even appointed her, considering "they have a hot potato on their

Sylvia Earle in
Her Own Words

A Conversation with Sylvia Earle by Milbry Polk

POLK: What has life as an explorer under the sea taught you?

EARLE: Spending many hours under the ocean has impressed on me that we are a part of nature, not apart from nature. The view from within the sea complements the view from space, showing all of us that from afar the world is mostly blue and from deep within, all that blue is more than just water. The ocean is filled with life that shapes the way the world works, generating oxygen, absorbing carbon dioxide, governing planetary chemistry.

POLK: What have been your greatest adventures?

EARLE: The greatest adventure is out there yet to happen. The next adventure is always the best one. But among the most memorable adventures for me so far have taken place during the years I have studied whales underwater, meeting them on their own terms, living underwater for extended periods of time in various underwater laboratories, and using more than 25 different submersibles to explore the deep sea. I have especially loved using the one-person subs, Deep Rover and Deep Worker, for solo dives to as much as 1000 meters deep around the coastline of the United States. Starting three companies from scratch was an adventure, for sure, especially "diving in" to everything from accounting and legal issues to engineering and marketing. There is great satisfaction developing an enterprise that works—and also makes a difference. One of my greatest adventures began in 1998 as Explorer in Residence at the National Geographic, dreaming up [programs], gaining support, and eventually involving thousands of participants in a program using various ships and Deep Worker subs in a program of research, exploration and education in America's marine sanctuaries.

The greatest adventure of all, though, has been having children and now grandchildren, and sharing the excitement of their discoveries.

POLK: How deep under the sea were you when you lived there?
EARLE: Most underwater labs are at the same basic level—50 or 60 feet, including the ones I have used in Florida, the Bahamas and the Virgin Islands. Once I spent the night 20 feet underwater in the underwater hotel, Jules, in Key Largo.

POLK: Where did you swim with the whales?
EARLE: I have had the joy of swimming with humpback whales in Hawaii and Bermuda and with southern right whales in South Africa.

POLK: Could you hear them singing underwater?
EARLE: Oh, yes—the humpbacks, anyway. They have a wonderful repetoire of sounds and the best place to hear them is under the ocean.

POLK: What projects are you involved with now?
EARLE: Presently I am continuing as Explorer in Residence at the National Geographic Society and as the Chairman of Deep Ocean Exploration and Research (DOER) with my daughter and son-in-law—a family enterprise. I am also serving as the Executive Director of Global Ocean Programs for Conservation International and Program Director for the Harte Research Institute at Texas A&M for research, exploration, and education concerning the Gulf of Mexico. I am President of Common Heritage Corporation, a Hawaiian organization focusing on water and energy issues, and I serve on the board of Kerr McGee as well as more than a dozen non-profit institutions. Some might say "too many irons, not enough fire," but I keep stoking the fire, hoping to accomplish as much as possible with the time I have, and igniting as many partners as I can enlist.

POLK: Tell us about your exploration company, DOER.
EARLE: DOER designs, develops, and operates equipment for access and work underwater. Technologies already available are used when possible, and when necessary, new systems are created. We do what it takes to solve problems, mostly in the ocean, but sometimes in strange places—such as the tunnel draining ground water under the city of Austin, Texas. Projects in the last few years have ranged from work with the navy at the North Pole to tropical reefs in Micronesia and deep water operations searching for giant squids in New Zealand.

POLK: What kinds of challenges technologically is ocean exploration faced with today?

EARLE: The biggest problems, I believe, are not technological, but philosophical. Technology exists that could achieve much more than is now being done, but the resources needed are in short supply. Many seem to think the ocean has already been explored, and others just seem not to care. For example, technology exists that would make it possible to gain access to full ocean depth, seven miles down, but no system exists that can do so. In 1960, the two-person bathyscape, *Trieste*, made the descent once for half an hour, and in recent years, a Japanese robot has been deployed for hours of observations. That robot was recently lost, however. That means that a part of the ocean as large as the United States or Australia or China is not accessible to humankind.

POLK: What are your personal goals?

EARLE: My goals now are much the same as they have been for most of my life—as a scientist to learn everything I can about the ocean, and then to try to inspire people to care about the natural systems upon which we are all dependent. I want people to appreciate the natural world, the source of our health, wealth, survival, and well-being.

POLK: What is the greatest challenge ahead for us?

EARLE: The most urgent goal is to find an enduring place for ourselves within the natural systems that sustain us. We have a big job to do to restore damage already done and to protect what remains of the world's support systems—land, air, and water, as well as the living matrix of life that makes the world hospitable for the likes of us.

POLK: Where are the critical endangered areas in the oceans and why?

EARLE: Coastal areas near large cities worldwide are most affected, but the entire ocean is being stressed and degraded by the millions of tons of trash and toxic wastes that are being dumped in and by the millions of tons of wildlife that are being extracted.

POLK: What kind of actions could individuals take now that might help make a difference?

EARLE: I suggest that individuals look in the mirror—consider their talents—then use them to make a difference. Everyone has power. The trick is, to use that power effectively. It may be something as simple as showing a child the wonders of a seashell, or as complex as getting a government agency to change its policies in favor of ocean care. To make a difference concerning overfishing and the damage it is causing, I have personally stopped eating seafood. Popular food fish such as swordfish, tuna, sharks, and grouper survive today in terrifyingly low numbers compared to what they were when I was a child.

POLK: What words of advice do you have for those interested in learning about or making a career of oceanography?
Earle: Follow your dreams. You don't have to be an oceanographer to care about the ocean. As a resident of the blue planet, everyone should become acquainted with the nature of the aquatic systems that shape our lives. Learning about the natural systems that sustain us should be as basic as learning our ABC's and numbers. Poetry, music, art, policy, history, archaeology, engineering, photography, medicine, marketing—it's hard to imagine an aspect of human endeavor that does not relate to the sea, one way or another. If you DO aspire to be an oceanographer, don't be discouraged by those who say that you can't make a living at it. Take school seriously and acquire all the knowledge you can about the aspects of the ocean that appeal to you the most, whether it's geology, chemistry, physics, biology, or whatever. Go get wet! As important as classrooms are, the best teacher, the best university, the finest laboratory is the ocean itself.

Series Consulting Editor Milbry Polk spoke with Sylvia Earle in July 2003.

Anton Bruun has had a colorful history. Originally called *Aras*, the ship was launched as a private yacht in 1930. It served in World War II as the USS *Williamsburg* and then, in 1945, replaced *Potomac* as the presidential yacht. The National Science Foundation refitted the ship for oceanographic research in 1962, and over the next two years, as *Anton Bruun*, it made nine trips to the Indian Ocean. Its oceanographic voyages continued until 1968. This photograph of Earle was taken on an expedition to Chile in 1965.

The Spanish explorer Juan Ponce de Léon named the Tortuga Islands for the vast population of turtles he found there; the islands later became known as the Dry Tortugas because they offer no fresh water. But the area, located off of Florida's southwestern coast, remains rich in sea life, and its extensive coral reefs are an important site of maritime research. The Sustainable Seas Expedition conducted three deep-water surveys there between 1997 and 2002.

Earle and her daughter, Elizabeth Taylor, on one of the Hydrolab missions in the Bahamas, 1975. Hydrolab was designed in 1966 and began to support shallow-water research missions four years later. Over the next fifteen years, it became the NOAA's principal undersea research facility in the Caribbean and hosted hundreds of international

researchers. According to Elizabeth Taylor, Tektite was like a hotel, but the smaller Hydrolab was "like underwater camping." "While Sylvia was in the Hydrolab for seven to fourteen days," Taylor recalls, "I worked on the surface support crew, monitoring the radio at night and taking supplies down to the habitat during the day." NOAA decommissioned Hydrolab in 1985 and replaced it with the Aquarius project in the Florida Keys.

The basket starfish earns its name by extending a "basket" of branches into the current. The branches wrap around small prey, and their tiny hooks hold the starfish's catch in place. The process depends on darkness; in excessive light, the starfish curls defensively into a ball. Earle examined this specimen in 1978.

In Catalina, Earle studied life in the undersea kelp forests; she investigated this sea hare in 1979. Like the squid, most varieties of sea hare can release a cloud of "ink." It is commonly believed that this confuses potential attackers and enables the hare to escape, but the creature moves too slowly for escape to be an option. Sea hares do seem to store poisonous chemicals, though, which they release when threatened.

In 1981, Earle and Graham Hawkes founded two design companies to analyze and overcome the problems of deep-sea exploration. One of their first designs was *Deep Rover* (shown here), a "mid-water" vehicle that reached depths of about three thousand feet. It included sensory systems so sophisticated that its operators could "feel" objects underwater and manipulate them as if with their own hands. Earle considered this essential. In a submersible without manipulation, she once said, "you sort of scratch on the glass like a child in a candy store with no nickel." *Deep Rover* is still in operation.

Although it sometimes resembles the vegetable, the sea cucumber is actually an animal, in the same class as the starfish, the sea urchin, the sand dollar, and others. Its more than 1,200 species can be found throughout the world, particularly along the coastlines of Great Britain, Western Europe, and New England. Its eggs feed many other sea creatures, and its movement and feeding patterns help to recycle the ocean's nutrients. Still, the sea cucumber is known primarily for its unusual defense mechanism—abruptly expelling its innards, which regenerate easily.

Earle with one of the family pets, Blue Prints, on a trail near their home in Oakland, California. Earle's daughter Elizabeth recalls that, although Earle gave the dog to Graham Hawkes, "dogs being sensible creatures, Blue immediately bonded to Sylvia." Friendly relationships with animals like Blue Prints and the dolphin Sandy seem to have come easily to Earle since her earliest years.

hands."[77] Earle told reporters at the time of her resignation that although official intentions were good, neither funds nor action had materialized. "The inaction of good people is more devastating than the evil actions of a few," she said pointedly.[78] For Earle, a return to the private sector meant that she no longer had to mince words and publicly support government policy. Working in business in science and technology and writing books and articles for the popular media would allow her to assume her own voice as a passionate individual who knew the ocean from the inside out and knew that drastic steps had to be taken to save its future.

There was one other big reason she needed to leave the life of the bureaucracy. "I was suffering from dry rot," she told the editor of *National Wildlife* magazine. "I wanted to spend more time at sea."[79]

9

Hero of
the Planet
1992–2003

We have an opportunity, now, to achieve for humankind a
prosperous, enduring future. If we fail . . . our kind might well
be a passing phenomenon . . .

—Sylvia Earle, *Sea Change:*
A Message of the Oceans

A PARTIAL SOLUTION

Sylvia Earle may have left her post at NOAA, but she did not stop thinking of strategies to protect the world's oceans. She continued to work as a consultant to NOAA, traveling with 140 other scientists from around the world for three months aboard NOAA's research vessel, *Mt. Mitchell,* to study the damage and potential for restoration in the Persian Gulf. For Earle and many others, that situation presented an urgent argument for the creation of marine sanctuaries throughout the world.

In a paper coauthored with two NOAA scientists—marine sanctuary advocate Francesca Cava and hazardous waste expert John Robinson—Earle described the precious ecosystem of the Persian Gulf. She called it the "shallow, highly productive sea that has, over the ages, been a significant factor in shaping the direction of the region's human development." The vast shallows of the Persian Gulf supported plant life, from micro-algae to sea-grass meadows, marshes, and mangroves. "The rich communities of marine organisms also attract millions of birds," the three scientists wrote, noting that temperatures and water salinity brought distinctive species to the Gulf area. Mudflat samples before the war revealed "several hundred thousand small invertebrates in six or more phyla per square meter sampled." These tiny species provided food for larger sea creatures of benefit to human beings in the form of "productive commercial invertebrate fisheries, including pearl oysters, crabs, squids, ten shrimp species, and at least two kinds of lobsters."[80] Fifty-seven different kinds of coral reef species were identified in the Persian Gulf as well. The Persian Gulf was a precious body of water, well worth protecting.

Cava, Robinson, and Earle proposed that the Gulf be designated a marine sanctuary. Setting up such sanctuaries was a concept already in place in the United States and elsewhere. The U.S. Congress had passed the Marine Sanctuaries Act in 1972, allowing the government to identify "areas of special national significance due to their resources or human use values with reference to conservation, recreation, ecological, historical, educational or aesthetic qualities."[81] Through an "integrated ecosystem management approach," as Earle and her coauthors called it,[82] governments could monitor human activities that affect the watery realm. They could restrict the harvest of fish and other sea life, and regulate industrial development and practices nearby.

It would take an international effort to develop a marine sanctuary in the Persian Gulf. Representatives from countries bordering its waters had already formed the Regional Organization for the Protection of the Marine Environment (ROPME), with headquarters in Kuwait. The National Commission on Wildlife Conservation and Development of the Kingdom of Saudi Arabia had already proposed protecting a few specific areas within the Gulf. Although the dream of an internationally recognized marine sanctuary never materialized, since the early 1990s, several delicate regions throughout the Persian Gulf have come under government protection. Among these protected areas are Lebanon's Palm Island Marine Reserve, Saudi Arabia's Al-Jubail Marine Sanctuary, and Oman's Ra's Al-Hadd Sea Turtle Reserve.[83]

BACK TO HER OWN MESSAGE

In the intense activity surrounding her government post, Sylvia Earle and Graham Hawkes had decided to divorce. "I was always trying to combine everything, combine science and traditional expectation," she told Peggy Orenstein of *New York Times Magazine* in 1991. "But it's repeatedly been my choice to opt for a career as a scientist. . . . It's who and what I am, fundamentally, beyond being a woman, beyond being a wife or beyond being a mother. It's just who I am."

Earle began to write a book in which she would weave together two themes: her own evolution as a diver, a scientist, and a friend of the ocean, and mounting world concerns over ocean habitats falling victim to human greed and progress. *Sea Change: A Message of the Oceans* was published by Putnam in 1995 and was quickly recognized as a "superior book about the sea and our planet and us," as a reviewer for the *Boston Globe* put it. A fellow explorer, Dr. Jane Goodall, called it a "landmark book of tremendous importance."[84]

"I want to share the exhilaration of discovery, and convey a sense of urgency about the need for all of us to use whatever talents and resources we have to continue to explore and under-stand the nature of this extraordinary ocean planet," Earle wrote in the book's introduction. "Far and away the greatest threat to the sea and to the future of mankind is ignorance."[85] Her mission was clear: to educate her fellow citizens of the world about the plenitude and significance of the ocean and to sensitize all people to its vulnerability. She retold the fable of the goose that laid the golden egg. Its owner, a greedy farmer, wanted more than one golden egg a day and cut open the goose, "only to end up with . . . a dead goose." Like that farmer, wrote Earle,

> We are blessed with a wondrous source of wealth, the oceans. Presently, however, humankind is insisting on taking more than a sustainable supply of golden eggs; feathers are being plucked, and some have begun to carve into meat and bone. . . .
>
> We have an opportunity, now, to achieve for humankind a prosperous, enduring future. If we fail, through inability to resolve thorny issues, or by default born of indifference, greed, or lack of knowledge, our kind might well be a passing short-term phenomenon, a mere three or four million–year blip in the ancient and ongoing saga of life on Earth.
>
> Traditionally, the sea has been regarded as the common heritage for all mankind. Now its care must be acknowledged as a common responsibility.[86]

A DIFFICULT YEAR, THEN A TRIUMPHANT YEAR

Years after, Sylvia Earle would look back and call 1997 "the worst year of my life." In January, a dear friend of hers died of cancer. A few weeks later, her mother—with whom she and her children had been very close all their lives—died as well. Then her great diving hero, Jacques-Yves Cousteau, died on June 24 at the age of 87. Asked to write his obituary for *Time* magazine, Sylvia Earle began by quoting the *National Geographic* article she had read as a teenager:

> "The best way to observe fish is to become a fish," wrote Jacques-Yves Cousteau in 1952. "And the best way to become a fish is to don an underwater breathing device called the Aqualung." Like many thousands of other humans-who-would-be-fish, I took his advice. . . . He touched our minds and hearts, luring us onward—and downward. While celebrating a life well lived, I personally mourn the loss of a trusted friend. Surely the sea does too.[87]

Into this period of mourning came new life when Earle's older daughter, Elizabeth, gave birth in June. Earle later recognized this birth of her third grandchild as a turning point, a new affirmation of life during a difficult year. Elizabeth and her family moved into Earle's Oakland home and helped run her business. "That gave me latitude to think about what else I wanted to do," said Earle.[88]

The following year, 1998, crowned many of Sylvia Earle's life-long efforts. She reestablished her relationship with the National Geographic Society and started working on a television documentary about the bluefin tuna. Also in the works was a new plan designed by the National Geographic Society to heighten public awareness about ongoing world explorations. Society officials named Sylvia Earle the organization's 1998 explorer-in-residence.

That appointment was only the beginning. Behind the scenes, Earle and National Geographic Society officials were discussing ways

In 1998, Earle helped found the Sustainable Seas Expedition, a five-year project whose goal was to explore the nation's twelve maritime sanctuaries. One point of concern at the time was coral bleaching. Corals have a symbiotic relationship with the algae that live within their cells. Corals are sensitive to their environment, and even slight variations in temperature or light can cause them to expel the algae from their tissues. This causes them to lose their color, and it can be fatal. Here, Earle checks for evidence of bleaching on a Sustainable Seas expedition in 2002.

to combine her vast knowledge of and unbridled passion for the oceans with the National Geographic Society's international influence. In April 1998, their plans coalesced in the Sustainable Seas Expedition, thanks to a $5-million-grant from the Richard and Rhoda Goldman Fund—the largest gift a foundation had ever made to the National Geographic Society. "The Goldman Fund award is breathtaking," Earle responded when the gift was announced. "People think we know what's under that big blue surface, but we don't." [89]

The Sustainable Seas initiative would include systematic explorations by manned submersible of America's marine sanctuaries. Expedition divers would install scientific instruments where humans had never made observations before, promising long-term readings of currents, temperatures, and other habitat features. Maps of the ocean floor and photographs of ocean communities would result as well. All this information, Earle explained, would contribute substantially to national and international understanding, leading to wiser ocean policies. "Our goal is an ethic of ocean stewardship similar to our stewardship of national parks, and eventually an international ethic that transcends laws."[90]

THE INTERNATIONAL YEAR OF THE OCEAN

Everything seemed to be lining up for the benefit of the ocean. The nation's newly elected leaders, President Bill Clinton and Vice President Al Gore, heard the urgent messages from ocean advocates like Sylvia Earle, and the White House declared that the United States would join other nations in observing 1998 as "The Year of the Ocean." A National Ocean Conference, the first in 25 years, was convened in June in Monterey, California. Not two weeks before, at the World Environment Day celebrations in Moscow, Russia, Sylvia Earle was inducted into the Global 500 Roll of Honor, earning a prestigious title awarded to those who had contributed the most to protecting the world's environment.

At the Monterey conference, she stood at the podium with her nation's top leaders. First Lady Hillary Rodham Clinton opened the meeting and introduced the National Geographic explorer-in-residence, Sylvia Earle, who addressed the audience briefly before introducing the next speaker, Vice President Al Gore. Later during the conference, President Bill Clinton spoke. He commended the promise of the National Geographic Sustainable Seas Expedition.

Not even all this publicity kept Earle above water. In August 1998, she joined six other scientists in a weeklong saturation dive in the Florida Keys. They lived in a habitat named *Aquarius,* placed 65 feet underwater near Conch Reef, off Key Largo, part of the recently established Florida Keys Marine Sanctuary. On Thursday, August 6, communication links to *Aquarius* allowed Earle to report on the mission's findings to John Fahey, president of the National Geographic Society. The American public listened in,

NATIONAL MARINE SANCTUARIES

In 1975, the United States established its first marine sanctuary, protecting a site discovered just two years earlier in Cape Hatteras, North Carolina. There, 16 miles offshore in 230 feet of water, lay the remains of the U.S.S. *Monitor,* the Civil War-era, iron-armored Union gunboat that sank in 1862. Although artifacts from the historic ship have been removed from the water for display in the Mariner's Museum in Newport News, Virginia, the hulk still lies on the ocean bottom, covered with algae and barnacles, a home for underwater life in multiple shapes and sizes.

Since 1975, a dozen more important underwater sites have been singled out for protection by law. Each harbors treasures integral to our nation's cultural and natural history. On the Flower Garden Banks, 110 miles off the coast of Texas and Louisiana in the Gulf of Mexico, coral reefs spawn under the full moon of August. The Hawaiian Islands Humpback Whale Sanctuary protects waters favored by whales for winter breeding. Thunder Bay, in northern Lake Ontario, contains more than 150 shipwrecks, artifacts from centuries of trade and travel on the Great Lakes waterways. The Gulf of the Farallones, northwest of San Francisco Bay, is a favorite destination for seals, sea lions, and seabirds by the thousands.

Sylvia Earle and photographer Wolcott Henry created a book about marine sanctuaries, *Wild Ocean: America's Parks Under the Seas.* The forward to the book, written by Vice President Al Gore, emphasized the meaning of these underwater treasures. Gore compared the sanctuaries to national parks and forests established a century before. "For ages," he wrote, "the seas have been a source of sustenance, solace, mystery, and awe. . . . Together, we can ensure that they are all this, and more, for generations to come."*

* Foreword, *Wild Ocean,* Washington: National Geographic Society, p. 7.

via transmission to NBC's *Today Show.* The occasion was cause for celebration, but the news was not. Far fewer fish were living on the reef, reported Earle, than she had observed just four years earlier.

Now the nation was listening. On Tuesday, September 29, 1998, Earle testified in Congress as one of three witnesses addressing the House Subcommittee on Fisheries Conservation, Wildlife, and Oceans. To present the Sustainable Seas project to the House subcommittee she screened a video produced by National Geographic. She advised the government to approach the seas with as much respect and curiosity as it had approached outer-space exploration. Once again, she urged that NOAA, like NASA, be made a more proactive springboard for science and discovery.

Days later, the October 5 issue of *Time* magazine hit the stands, declaring Sylvia Earle a "Hero for the Planet." "You have to love it before you are moved to save it," began the article, written by award-winning journalist Roger Rosenblatt.[91] He and Earle had spent several days together in California's Big Sur area, walking the rocky coastline, boating offshore, and visiting the Monterey Bay aquarium. "She is not always the easiest person to be with, especially at meals," wrote Rosenblatt. "One loses one's appetite for fish. She can rhapsodize about an Atlantic bluefin tuna until you not only regret every piece of bluefin sushi in your life, you also begin to see the tuna her way—as the lion of the deep."[92] Indeed, Earle had long before decided not to eat any wild seafood, and she encouraged others to change that one habit on behalf of the world's oceans.

PRESERVATION FOR COMING GENERATIONS

People around the world entered the year 1999 with a heightened sense of history and a fascination about the future. A century was coming to an end; a new millennium was about to begin. Calling the twentieth century the "Geographic Century," National Public Radio's *Morning Edition* ran a 40-week series profiling pioneers in the field, including Arctic explorer Robert Peary, Everest climber Edmund Hillary—and deep-sea diver

Sylvia Earle. The Library of Congress selected 83 Americans whom it considered "Living Legends." Again, the list included Sylvia Earle. On his NBC "Nightly News" show, Tom Brokaw singled out a handful of women to watch in the new millennium, among them Sylvia Earle. Despite all the attention, Earle did not swerve from the work at hand. In fact, she used the momentum to advance environmental causes.

Few adults and even fewer children can witness the underwater world firsthand, Earle recognized. To raise marine consciousness, she sought ways to communicate with the children of the nation and the world. She worked with editors at National Geographic to create two children's books. One—*Hello, Fish!*—was a simple picture book with colorful illustrations that invited children to observe and identify coral-reef creatures in their habitat. The other, *Dive! My Adventures in the Deep Frontier,* was a photographic book for older children. In this book, Earle shared her love, admiration, and concern for the world underwater by telling stories of some of her most memorable dives.

On Memorial Day weekend of 2000, President Bill Clinton stood on Maryland's Assateague Island National Seashore and proudly announced an array of new initiatives from his administration, all designed to protect the oceans and beaches of the United States of America. He thanked those in attendance who had so vehemently supported a strong government initiative in this matter. Among those he thanked was Sylvia Earle, whom he identified as "an explorer in residence for American citizens."[93]

The world's oceans, said President Clinton "are far more than a playground." The oceans and coastlines are "a storehouse of biodiversity," both "immensely powerful" but also "very, very fragile."[94] Since the 1998 National Ocean Conference, Clinton reported:

> We have quadrupled funding for national marine sanctuaries. We have new funding to rebuild our threatened

Earle and her children met this playful dolphin, Sandy, off San Salvador Island in 1976. "I have often looked longingly at the speed, agility, and gamboling grace of dolphins," Earle writes in *Sea Change*, "who sometimes fling themselves aloft with deliberate twists and spins that easily surpass the finest human gymnastic displays." It was the joy of moving like this, like a dolphin, that first attracted Earle to diving—and she has worked to communicate that joy ever since.

fisheries. We extended a moratorium on offshore oil leases for oil and gas drilling through 2012. We've been an international leader in efforts to protect whales and other endangered species. But we have to do more.[95]

He announced the establishment of ocean conservation zones, to be overseen by NOAA and the Environmental Protection Agency, and a new plan to protect the coral reefs of northwestern Hawaii.

Standing in the ocean air of Assateague, listening to the president of the United States speak of the importance of protecting the oceans, Sylvia Earle must have felt proud. Not only was the nation beginning to listen, but also people were beginning to take action. Many had asked her, "What can one person do?" Earle had shown them just how much one individual can accomplish. In the face of adversity and disaster, she had never given up. Now it looked as if her persistence might be making a difference.

TO EXPLORE AND TO PROTECT

Entering the twenty-first century, Sylvia Earle was recognized around the world as the ocean's best friend. Newly discovered marine life species, such as *Diadema sylvie,* a sea urchin, and *Pilina earli,* an underwater plant, had been named after her. *People Weekly* called her "the first lady of the sea" and "the Jacques Cousteau of our day."[96] The National Geographic Society revitalized its explorer-in-residence program, creating deeper, longer ties with explorers selected for the position. Sylvia Earle was one of the first seven named to the honor. The others included such luminaries as American historian Stephen Ambrose, chimpanzee expert Jane Goodall, and ethnobotanist of the Amazon Wade Davis. National Geographic Society President John Fahey set the tone for the new program by saying, "These days as we explore, the places and treasures we find are too often threatened with destruction. Today's explorer must also be a conservationist."[97] The mission suited Sylvia Earle very well.

REVIVING THE HORSESHOE CRAB

Through her business and her books, as well as her learned voice and her dynamic presence in the media and in the highest decision-making circles, Sylvia Earle was doing the most one person could do on behalf of the oceans. Her passion never flagged—either for her cause or for any opportunity to spend time underwater.

"In a very fundamental way, I'm changed forever because I lived underwater for two weeks in 1970," she reflected in 1989. "I wish that *everybody* could go live underwater, if only for a day."[98] If everyone did spend a day underwater, Earle believed, people would identify more closely with the plants and animals they saw there. They might come closer to thinking like a fish—something she had been doing most of her life.

"Ignorance," Earle said in 1999,

> is the single most frightening and dangerous threat to the health of the oceans. There is much to learn before it is possible to intelligently create a harmonious, viable place for ourselves on the planet. The best place to begin is by recognizing the magnitude of our ignorance, and not destroy species and natural systems we cannot recreate.[99]

A visit to the New Jersey beaches of her childhood revived her interest in a creature that had fascinated and intrigued her many years ago. In her book *Sea Change,* Earle described what she found:

> I noticed the glint of sunlight on something small and round, and gently lifted onto my fingertip a tiny, iridescent sphere. There, immersed in clear liquid inside a space smaller than a teardrop, was a miniature horseshoe crab,

with all the critical bits intact: rounded front end, oval eyes, leaflike gills, a small nub for a tail, and a priceless multimillion-year cargo of unique genetic information.[100]

Few others would have even noticed this little speck of life, let alone identified it by species or seen it as significant. Earle knew exactly what she was witnessing: the promise of life threatened by careless destruction. As she had done in her childhood, Earle gently returned the creature to the sea. The experience made her wonder, "What plan can we possibly devise that will ensure the continued, healthy functioning of a planet suitable for a relative newcomer, ourselves, if within decades we can render the place inhospitable for those who had endured the sweeping changes of the preceding few hundred thousand millennia?"[101]

Then, with a twist of perspective so characteristic of Sylvia Earle, she meditated further:

> Loss of horseshoe crabs might not seem like a big deal. I can imagine some of my cynical pals, drinking beer, munching pretzels, teasing me with killer questions, including the clincher: "Who cares? *I* don't!"
>
> I can also imagine a philosophical crab, perched on its several million-year track record of success, disdainfully reviewing our meager history . . . and thinking the same of us.[102]

Earle wanted to see the future take a different turn, guided by growing knowledge, respect, and care toward the ocean and the life within it. Believing that the survival of the planet depends on the health of its oceans and that the health of the oceans depends in large part on us, she has spent a lifetime trying to teach people to see from the perspective of the creatures of the deep.

Appendix

Air Pressure Below Sea Level

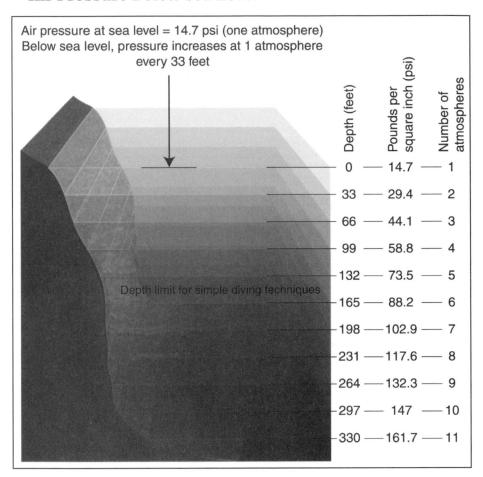

Air pressure at sea level = 14.7 psi (one atmosphere)
Below sea level, pressure increases at 1 atmosphere
every 33 feet

Depth (feet)	Pounds per square inch (psi)	Number of atmospheres
0	14.7	1
33	29.4	2
66	44.1	3
99	58.8	4
132	73.5	5
165	88.2	6
198	102.9	7
231	117.6	8
264	132.3	9
297	147	10
330	161.7	11

Depth limit for simple diving techniques

The air pressure exerted on the human body is 14.7 pounds per square inch (psi) at sea level, also called "one atmosphere" of pressure. As humans descend farther underwater, this pressure increases, causing the body to absorb gases, particularly oxygen and nitrogen, at a higher rate than normal. Divers must undergo decompression before returning to the surface, a process that allows their bodies to slowly adjust to the decreasing effects of air pressure on their bodies.

The Zones of the Ocean

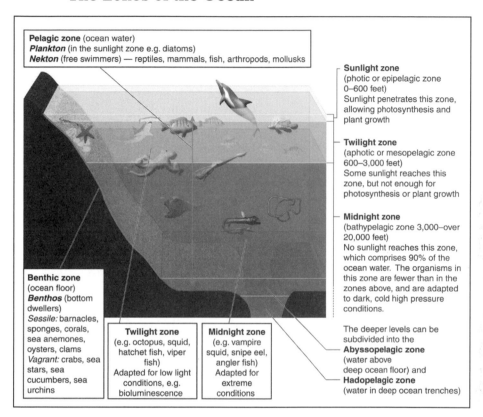

Pelagic zone (ocean water)
Plankton (in the sunlight zone e.g. diatoms)
Nekton (free swimmers) — reptiles, mammals, fish, arthropods, mollusks

Sunlight zone
(photic or epipelagic zone
0–600 feet)
Sunlight penetrates this zone,
allowing photosynthesis and
plant growth

Twilight zone
(aphotic or mesopelagic zone
600–3,000 feet)
Some sunlight reaches this
zone, but not enough for
photosynthesis or plant growth

Midnight zone
(bathypelagic zone 3,000–over
20,000 feet)
No sunlight reaches this zone,
which comprises 90% of the
ocean water. The organisms in
this zone are fewer than in the
zones above, and are adapted
to dark, cold high pressure
conditions.

Benthic zone
(ocean floor)
Benthos (bottom
dwellers)
Sessile: barnacles,
sponges, corals,
sea anemones,
oysters, clams
Vagrant: crabs, sea
stars, sea
cucumbers, sea
urchins

Twilight zone
(e.g. octopus, squid,
hatchet fish, viper
fish)
Adapted for low light
conditions, e.g.
bioluminescence

Midnight zone
(e.g. vampire
squid, snipe eel,
angler fish)
Adapted for
extreme
conditions

The deeper levels can be
subdivided into the
Abyssopelagic zone
(water above
deep ocean floor) and
Hadopelagic zone
(water in deep ocean trenches)

Scientists have divided the ocean into numerous zones according to the marine life that inhabits each layer of the sea. While Sylvia Earle's first underwater dive with breathing equipment only allowed her to reach 30 feet below the surface of the Weekiwatchee River, during her long career, Earle has dived to amazing depths. She lived in an underwater habitat during the Tektite project at 50 feet below sea level, took the submersible diving suit *Jim* down to 1,250 feet, and explored the Nankai Trough off the coast of Japan in the research submarine *Shinkai 6500* at more than 13,000 feet.

Chronology

1935 Sylvia Alice Earle is born.

1947 The Earle family moves to Gulf Coast of Florida.

1952 She takes her first dive, using a friend's father's helmet.

1953 Earle first uses Aqualung as student at Florida State University.

1954 She earns her B.A. from Florida State.

TIMELINE

1968
She joins Man-in-Sea Project; locks out of *Deep Diver* submersible in the Bahamas.

1979
Earle performs the deepest untethered solo dive in *Jim*; walks on Hawaii's ocean floor at 1,250 feet underwater.

1935
Sylvia Alice Earle is born.

1965–1967
Earle is resident director of Cape Haze Marine Laboratory, working with "shark lady" Eugenie Clark.

1964
She joins the research team on *Anton Bruun*, exploring Indian Ocean.

1930   1950   1960   1970

1952
She takes her first dive, using a friend's father's helmet.

1970
Earle leads an all-woman crew during two-week underwater research stay in Tektite II in the U.S. Virgin Islands.

1972–1975
Conducts five research missions in Hydrolab undersea laboratory.

1953
Earle first uses Aqualung as student at Florida State University.

1977
She spends months studying humpback whales in Hawaii and Alaska.

106

1955 She earns her M.S. from Duke University.

1957 Earle marries John Taylor.

1960 Her first child, Elizabeth Taylor, is born.

1962 Her second child, John Richie Taylor, is born.

1964 She joins the research team on *Anton Bruun,* exploring Indian Ocean.

1990–1992
Earle is appointed chief scientist, National Oceanic and Atmospheric Administration.

1998
She is named National Geographic Society's explorer-in-residence; speaks before historic National Ocean Conference; spearheads Sustainable Seas Expeditions, joint project of National Geographic and NOAA; is named a "Hero for the Planet" by *Time* magazine.

1981
With Graham Hawkes, she founds two companies: Deep Ocean Technology and Deep Ocean Engineering.

1980   1990   2000

1988
Earle dives in *Deep Rover* to 1,500 feet in Crater Lake, Oregon.

1992
Founds DOER, Deep Ocean Exploration and Research.

2000
Earle is named a Living Legend by the Library of Congress.

1989
In the wake of Exxon *Valdez* disaster, she visits site to assess environmental damage.

1991
Earle visits oil spills in Persian Gulf caused by retreating Iraqis during Desert Storm.

Chronology

1965–1967 Earle is resident director of Cape Haze Marine Laboratory, working with "shark lady" Eugenie Clark.

1966 She completes Ph.D. dissertation on algae, including inventory of underwater plants in the Gulf of Mexico, and it is published in scientific journal.

1966 Marries Giles Mead and moves to the Boston area.

1968 She joins Man-in-Sea Project; dives to 100 feet in the Bahamas.

1968 Her third child, Gale Mead, is born.

1970 She moves with husband and family to California.

1970 Earle leads all-woman crew during two-week underwater research stay in Tektite II in the U.S. Virgin Islands.

1971–1975 She participates in and directs numerous research dive and underwater-habitat expeditions around world.

1975 She dives Truk Lagoon's World War II–era wrecks with photographer Al Giddings.

1977 She spends months studying humpback whales in Hawaii and Alaska.

1979 Earle performs deepest untethered solo dive in *Jim;* walks on Hawaii's ocean floor at 1,250 feet underwater.

1980 She publishes first book, *Exploring the Deep Frontier.*

1981 With Graham Hawkes, she founds two companies: Deep Ocean Technology and Deep Ocean Engineering.

1984 Deep Ocean Engineering's *Deep Rover* is launched.

1985 Deep Ocean Engineering's *Phantom* is developed.

1986 Earle marries Graham Hawkes.

1988 Earle dives in *Deep Rover* to bottom of Crater Lake, Oregon.

1989 In wake of Exxon *Valdez* disaster, she visits site to assess environmental damage.

1990–1992   Earle is appointed chief scientist, National Oceanic and Atmospheric Administration, and end her involvement with Deep Ocean Engineering.

1991   Earle visits oil spills in Persian Gulf resulting when Iraqis retreat during Desert Storm.

1992   After leaving her NOAA post, she founds Deep Ocean Exploration and Research.

1995   She publishes *Sea Change: A Message of the Oceans.*

1998   She is named National Geographic Society's explorer-in-residence for the year; speaks before historic National Ocean Conference; spearheads Sustainable Seas Expeditions, joint project of National Geographic and NOAA; is named a "Hero for the Planet" by *Time* magazine.

1999   Earle publishes *Wild Ocean: America's Parks Under the Seas.*

2000   She is named one of seven National Geographic Society explorers-in-residence; named a Living Legend by the Library of Congress.

Notes

Chapter 1

1. Sylvia A. Earle, *Sea Change: A Message of the Oceans*. New York: Ballantine Books, 1995, pp. 106–107.

2. Quoted in Earle, *Sea Change*, p. 52.

3. Sylvia A. Earle and Al Giddings, *Exploring the Deep Frontier: The Adventure of Man in the Sea*. Washington, D.C.: National Geographic Society, 1980, p. 230.

4. Earle, *Sea Change*, p. 107.

5. Ibid.

6. Ibid., p. 109.

7. Ibid.

8. Ibid., p. 120.

9. Ibid., p. 121.

Chapter 2

10. Quoted in "Sylvia Earle, Ph.D., Undersea Explorer," interview in "The Hall of Science & Exploration," Academy of Achievement Web site, *http://www.achievement.org*.

11. Quoted in William White, "Her Deepness," *New Yorker*, July 3, 1989, p. 47.

12. Quoted in "Sylvia Earle, Ph.D."

13. Quoted in White, "Her Deepness," p. 47.

14. Quoted in "Sylvia Earle, Ph.D."

15. Quoted in White, "Her Deepness," pp. 49–50.

16. Quoted in "Sylvia Earle, Ph.D."

17. All quotations from Sylvia A. Earle, *Sea Change: A Message of the Oceans*. New York: Fawcett Columbine/Bantam Books, 1995, pp. xx–xxi.

18. Quoted in "Sylvia Earle, Ph.D."

19. As explained by Sylvia Earle in *Sea Change*, p. 205.

20. Both quoted in Earle, *Sea Change*, pp. 237–238.

21. From William Beebe, *Beneath Tropic Seas: A Record of Diving Among the Coral Reefs of Haiti*, New York/London: G. P. Putnam's Sons, 1928, p. 3.

22. Captain Jacques-Yves Cousteau, "Fish Men Explore a New World Undersea," *National Geographic Magazine*, October, 1952, p. 431.

23. Earle, *Sea Change*, p. 41.

24. Ibid., p. 43.

Chapter 3

25. In Earle and Giddings, *Exploring the Deep Frontier*, p. 25.

26. Earle, *Sea Change*, p. 45.

27. Ibid., pp. 46–47.

28. Ibid., p. 47.

29. Quoted in Peggy Orenstein, "Champion of the Deep," *New York Times Magazine*, June 23, 1991, p. 18.

30. Quoted in White, "Her Deepness," p. 50.

31. Ibid.

32. Earle, *Sea Change*, p. 26.

Chapter 4

33. Quoted in Earle, *Sea Change*, pp. 26–27.

34. As discussed in Anwar Abdel Aleem, "Reminiscences of the Indian Ocean," *Southampton Oceanography Centre* website, *http://www.soc.soton.ac.uk/OTHERS/CSMS/OCHAL/iocean.htm*

35. Earle, *Sea Change,* p. 54.

36. Quoted in White, "Her Deepness," pp. 50–51.

37. Quoted in Earle, *Sea Change,* pp. 60–61.

38. Quoted in Earle and Giddings, *Exploring the Deep Frontier,* p. 168.

Chapter 5
39. Ibid., p. 140.

40. Ibid., pp. 139–140.

41. Ibid., p. 141.

42. Bruce B. Collette, "Conclusions," in *Results of the Tektite Program: Ecology of Coral Reef Fishes,* Natural History Museum, Los Angeles County, Science Bulletin 14, 1972, p. 174.

43. Ibid.

44. As explained in Earle and Giddings, *Exploring the Deep Frontier,* p. 142.

45. Quoted in White, "Her Deepness," p. 53.

46. Ibid., p. 54.

Chapter 6
47. Sylvia A. Earle, Ph.D., "Life Springs From Death in Truk Lagoon," *National Geographic,* May 1976, p. 582.

48. Ibid., p. 583.

49. Ibid., p. 586.

50. Ibid.

51. Quoted in White, "Her Deepness," p. 56.

52. Ibid.

53. Sylvia A. Earle, Ph.D., "Humpbacks: The Gentle Whales," *National Geographic,* January 1979, p. 2.

54. Ibid.

55. Earle, *Sea Change,* p. 97.

56. Quoted in White, "Her Deepness," p. 58.

Chapter 7
57. Earle and Giddings, *Exploring the Deep Frontier,* p. 8.

58. Earle, *Sea Change,* p. 128.

59. Ibid., p. 132.

60. White, "Her Deepness," p. 56.

Chapter 8
61. Ibid., p. 50.

62. Earle, *Sea Change,* p. 254.

63. Reported by Earle in *Sea Change,* p. 256.

64. Reported by Earle in *Sea Change,* p. 257.

65. White, "Her Deepness," p. 63.

66. Ibid., p. 64.

67. Ibid., p. 44.

68. Earle, *Sea Change,* p. 265.

69. Earle, *Sea Change,* p. 271.

70. White, "Her Deepness," p. 71.

71. Statistics discussed in Earle, *Sea Change,* p. 185.

72. "An Environmentalist's Take on War," interview with Jonathan Lash, director of the World Resources Institute, January 10, 2003, MSNBC Web site, *http://www.msnbc.com/new/ 856185.asp?cp1=1#BODY.*

Notes

73. Quoted in Orenstein, "Champion of the Deep," p. 31.

74. Ibid.

75. Article by Keith Schneider, *New York Times,* April 1, 1991, p. A–1.

76. "Chief Scientist at Federal Agency to Resign," *New York Times,* January 19, 1992, p. A–18.

77. John McCosker, marine scientist at the California Academy of Sciences, quoted in Mark Wexler, "Sylvia Earle's Excellent Adventure," *National Wildlife,* April–May 1999.

78. Ibid.

79. Wexler, "Sylvia Earle's Excellent Adventure."

Chapter 9

80. Ibid.

81. Congressional definition of "marine sanctuaries," as quoted in Francesca M. Cava, John H. Robinson, and Sylvia A. Earle, "Should the Arabian (Persian) Gulf become a marine sanctuary?" *Oceanus,* Fall 1993, vol. 36, no. 3, pp. 53–63.

82. Ibid.

83. "Biodiversity," accessed on *Global Environment Outlook 2000,* United Nations Environment Programme Web site *http://www.grida.no/geo2000/english/0109.htm*

84. As quoted in paperback edition of *Sea Change,* front matter.

85. Earle, *Sea Change,* p. xxi.

86. Ibid., p. 328.

87. Sylvia Earle, "O captain, my captain," *Time,* July 7, 1997, p. 25.

88. Quoted in Cathy Healy, "Sylvia Earle tells Lunch Forum about NGS's efforts to create underwater national parks," National Geographic Society press release, October 7, 1998.

89. Quoted in Margaret Sears, "Goldman Fund grant assures Society a leading role in deep-ocean research," *Connections,* National Geographic Society, June 1998.

90. Ibid.

91. Roger Rosenblatt, "Call of the Sea," *Time,* October 5, 1998, p. 57.

92. Ibid., p. 61.

93. Bill Clinton, "Remarks by the President on Protecting the Oceans," May 26, 2000, Office of the Press Secretary, The White House, reprinted by Cathy Healy, National Geographic Society public relations, June 2, 2000.

94. Ibid., pp. 2–3.

95. Ibid., p. 3.

96. "Depth Charger: First Lady of the sea Sylvia Earle dives in to save the world's polluted oceans," *People Weekly,* March 6, 2000, p. 159.

97. Cathy Healy, "Seven pioneers to gather to redefine exploration," National Geographic Society press release, April 6, 2000.

98. Quoted in White, "Her Deepness," p. 56.

99. Quoted in Bruce Lavendel, "Her Royal Deepness," *Animals* (the magazine of the Massachusetts Society of the Prevention of Cruelty to Animals), March 1999, p. 36.

100. Earle, *Sea Change,* p. 244.

101. Ibid.

102. Ibid.

Bibliography

Beebe, William. *Beneath Tropic Seas: A Record of Diving Among the Coral Reefs of Haiti.* New York/London: G. P. Putnam's Sons, 1928.

Carson, Rachel. *The Sea Around Us.* New York: Signet, 1961.

Cava, Francesca M., John H. Robinson, and Sylvia A. Earle. "Should the Arabian (Persian) Gulf become a marine sanctuary?" *Oceanus,* vol. 36, no. 3 (Fall 1993): 53–63.

"Chief Scientist at Federal Agency to Resign." *New York Times,* January 19, 1992, sec. A.

Clinton, Bill. "Remarks by the President on Protecting the Oceans." May 26, 2000, Office of the Press Secretary, The White House.

Collette, Bruce B. and Sylvia A. Earle, eds. *Results of the Tektite Program: Ecology of Coral Reef Fishes.* Natural History Museum, Los Angeles County, Science Bulletin 14, 1972.

Cousteau, Jacques-Yves. "Fish Men Explore a New World Undersea." *National Geographic,* October 1952.

"Depth Charger: First Lady of the Sea Sylvia Earle Dives in to Save the World's Polluted Oceans." *People Weekly,* March 6, 2000.

Earle, Sylvia A. "Life Springs From Death in Truk Lagoon." *National Geographic,* May 1976.

———. "Humpbacks: The Gentle Whales." *National Geographic,* January 1979.

———. "A Walk in the Deep." *National Geographic,* May 1980.

———. *Sea Change: A Message of the Oceans.* New York: Ballantine Books, 1995.

———. "O Captain, My Captain." *Time,* July 7, 1997.

Earle, Sylvia A., and Al Giddings. *Exploring the Deep Frontier: The Adventure of Man in the Sea.* Washington, D.C.: National Geographic Society, 1980.

Earle, Sylvia A., and Robert J. Lavenberg, eds. *Results of the Tektite Program: Coral Reef Invertebrates and Plants.* Natural History Museum of Los Angeles County, Science Bulletin 20, June 30, 1975.

Earle, Sylvia A., and Wolcott Henry. *Wild Ocean: America's Parks Under the Sea.* Washington: National Geographic Society, 1999.

Healy, Cathy. "Sylvia Earle Tells Lunch Forum About NGS's Efforts to Create Underwater National Parks." National Geographic Society, Press Release, October 7, 1998.

———. "Seven Pioneers to Gather to Redefine Exploration." National Geographic Society, Press Release, April 6, 2000.

Lavendel, Bruce. "Her Royal Deepness." *Animals* (the magazine of the Massachusetts Society of the Prevention of Cruelty to Animals), March 1999.

Orenstein, Peggy. "Champion of the Deep." *New York Times Magazine,* June 23, 1991.

Rosenblatt, Roger. "Call of the Sea." *Time,* October 5, 1998.

Schneider, Keith. "U.S. Says Harm from Valdez Spill is Much Worse than was Thought." *New York Times,* April 1, 1991, sec. A.

Sears, Margaret. "Goldman Fund Grant Assures Society a Leading Role in Deep-Ocean Research." *Connections,* National Geographic Society, June 1998.

Wexler, Mark. "Sylvia Earle's Excellent Adventure." *National Wildlife,* April–May 1999.

White, William. "Her Deepness." *New Yorker,* July 3, 1989.

Websites

Aleem, Anwar Abdel. "Reminiscences of the Indian Ocean." *Southampton Oceanography Centre* Website, http://www.soc.soton.ac.uk/OTHERS/CSMS/OCHAL/iocean.htm

Earle, Sylvia. "Sylvia Earle, Ph.D., Undersea Explorer: Interview in The Hall of Science & Exploration," Academy of Achievement Website, http://www.achievement.org

———. "An Environmentalist's Take on War: Interview with Sylvia Earle, conducted by Jonathan Lash, director of the World Resources Institute, January 10, 2003, MSNBC Website, http://www.msnbc.com/new/856185.asp?cp1=1#BODY

Florida State Department of Oceanography Newsletter Website, No. 20, Spring/Summer 2000, "Alumni Notes," http://www.ocean.fsu.edu/~www/newsletter/ SPRSUM00/alumninotes.html

Global Environment Outlook 2000, United Nations Environment Programme Website, http://www.grida.no/geo2000/english/0109.htm

Further Reading

Books

Ballard, Robert D. *Adventures in Ocean Exploration: From the Discovery of the Titanic to the Search for Noah's Flood.* Washington: National Geographic, 2001.

Beebe, William. *Half Mile Down.* New York: Harcourt, Brace and Co., 1934.

Byatt, Andrew, Alastair Fothergill, and Martha Holmes. *Blue Planet.* New York: DK Publishing, 2002.

Clark, Eugenie. *Lady with a Spear.* New York: Harper & Brothers, 1953.

Cousteau, Jacques. *The Silent World.* New York: Harper & Brothers, 1953.

———. *The Ocean World.* New York: Abradale Press, 1985.

Earle, Sylvia A. *National Geographic Atlas of the Ocean: The Deep Frontier.* Washington: National Geographic Society, 2001.

Ellis, Richard. *The Empty Ocean.* Washington: Shearwater Books, 2003.

Gore, Al. *Earth in the Balance: Ecology and the Human Spirit.* New York: Houghton Mifflin, 1990.

Kahari, Victoria. *Water Baby: The Story of Alvin.* New York: Oxford University Press, 1990.

Macinnis, Joseph, ed. *Saving the Oceans.* Toronto, Canada: Firefly Books, 1996.

Piccard, J. and R. Dietz. *Seven Miles Down.* New York: G. P. Putnam's Sons, 1961.

Vanstrum, Glenn. *The Saltwater Wilderness.* New York: Oxford University Press, 2003.

Websites

Aquarius, NOAA's Underwater Laboratory
  http://www.uncw.edu/aquarius/

Subsea Robotics and Submersible Systems
  http://www.doermarine.com

National Geographic Society Explorers-in-Residence
  http://www.nationalgeographic.com/council/eir/index.html

National Marine Sanctuaries
  http://www.sanctuaries.nos.noaa.gov

National Undersea Research Program.
  http://www.nurp.noaa.gov

PADI (Professional Association of Diving Instructors)
  http://www.padi.com

Ocean Planet, a Smithsonian Institution Exhibition
  http://seawifs.gsfc.nasa.gov/ocean_planet.htm

Wetlands, Oceans & Watersheds, Environmental Protection Agency
  http://www.epa.gov/owow/

Woods Hole Oceanographic Institution
  http://www.whoi.edu

Index

Index

Index

Index

Index

Index

page:

3: Courtesy of DOER (Deep Ocean Exploration and Research)

8: Courtesy of DOER (Deep Ocean Exploration and Research)

15: Courtesy of DOER (Deep Ocean Exploration and Research)

22: Courtesy of DOER (Deep Ocean Exploration and Research)

29: Courtesy of DOER (Deep Ocean Exploration and Research)

34: Courtesy of DOER (Deep Ocean Exploration and Research)

39: Courtesy of DOER (Deep Ocean Exploration and Research)

43: Courtesy of DOER (Deep Ocean Exploration and Research)

57: Courtesy of DOER (Deep Ocean Exploration and Research)

59: Courtesy of DOER (Deep Ocean Exploration and Research)

62: Courtesy of DOER (Deep Ocean Exploration and Research)

69: Courtesy of DOER (Deep Ocean Exploration and Research)

74: Courtesy of DOER (Deep Ocean Exploration and Research)

81: Courtesy of DOER (Deep Ocean Exploration and Research)

86: Courtesy of DOER (Deep Ocean Exploration and Research)

95: Courtesy of DOER (Deep Ocean Exploration and Research)

100: Courtesy of DOER (Deep Ocean Exploration and Research)

TIPIN

All photos Courtesy of DOER (Deep Ocean Exploration and Research)

APPENDIX

Illustrations © Peter Lamb

Cover: Courtesy of DOER

Contributors

Susan Tyler Hitchcock is a nature lover and sailor. Two of her books, *Gather Ye Wild Things* and *Wildflowers on the Windowsill*, explore the botany, lore, and uses of wild plants. With her husband and two small children, she spent a year sailing in the Caribbean and wrote of that adventure in her book *Coming About: A Family Passage at Sea*. She also wrote *The University of Virginia: A Pictorial History*. She holds a B.A. and M.A. in English from the University of Michigan and a Ph.D. in English from the University of Virginia. She works as a freelance writer and editor from her mountainside home in Covesville, Virginia.

Series consulting editor **Milbry Polk** graduated from Harvard in 1976. An explorer all her life, she has ridden horseback through Pakistan's Northwest Territories, traveled with Bedouin tribesmen in Jordan and Egypt, surveyed Arthurian sites in Wales, and trained for the first Chinese-American canoe expedition. In 1979, supported by the National Geographic Society, Polk led a camel expedition retracing the route of Alexander the Great across Egypt.

Her work as a photojournalist has appeared in numerous magazines, including Time, Fortune, Cosmopolitan and Quest. Currently she is a contributing editor to the *Explorers Journal*. Polk is a Fellow of the Royal Geographic Society and a Fellow of the Explorers Club. She is the also the author of two award-winning books, *Egyptian Mummies* (Dutton Penguin, 1997) and *Women of Discovery* (Clarkson Potter, 2001).

Milbry Polk serves as an advisor to the George Polk Awards for Journalistic Excellence, is on the Council of the New York Hall of Science, serves on the Board of Governors of the National Arts Club, the Children's Shakespeare Theater Board and is the director of Wings World Quest. She lives in Palisades, New York, with her husband and her three daughters. She and her daughters row on the Hudson River.

Acknowledgment

Sincere gratitude is due to Dr. Sylvia Earle and her daughter, Elizabeth Taylor, for their generous contributions to this book.